THE COMPLETE
DIABETIC DIET AFTER 50

110+ Easy, Low-Sugar and Low-Carbs Recipes

for Living a Long, Healthy Life Without Sacrificing Taste.

Meal Plan and Diabetic Dessert Included

Robert Kevin Edwards

Credit: cover pics: @freepik.com

Medical Disclaimer

The content presented in this book is designed solely for informative reasons and should not be considered a replacement for expert medical guidance, diagnosis, or treatment. It is imperative to consult a physician or other trained healthcare expert for any inquiries pertaining to a medical condition or treatment.

The author of this publication lacks professional medical credentials and refrains from dispensing medical counsel. The author bears no liability for any inaccuracies or exclusions found within the content of this publication.

The user is advised that assuming any reliance on the information presented in this book is entirely their own responsibility.

PART 1: THE PATHOLOGY

What exactly is diabetes?

Diabetes is a chronic disease that affects how the body converts sustenance to energy. Normally, the body converts carbohydrate-containing foods into glucose, a type of sugar. Your pancreas then secretes insulin, a hormone that enables your cells to use glucose for energy.

Diabetes occurs when the body either does not produce enough insulin or does not use insulin effectively. This causes glucose levels to rise in the circulation. High blood sugar levels can cause nerve, blood vessel, and organ injury over time.

There are three primary varieties of diabetes:

- Type 1 diabetes is an autoimmune disease that causes the pancreas' insulin-producing cells to be attacked and destroyed.
- Type 2 diabetes is the most prevalent form of diabetes, characterized by insulin resistance or insufficient insulin production.
- Diabetes that develops during pregnancy.

What effects does diabetes have on the body?

Numerous body regions can sustain harm from high blood sugar levels, including:

Diabetes can result in pain, tingling, and paralysis in the hands, feet, and legs due to nerve damage throughout the body. Additionally, this may result in digestive, urinary, and sexual dysfunction.

Diabetes can impede blood vessels, reducing their flexibility and increasing their rigidity. This may increase the risk of cardiovascular disease, stroke, and kidney disease.

Diabetes can impair the blood vessels in the retina, the light-sensitive tissue at the back of the eye. This could lead to blindness.

And it can still cause damage to the kidneys, impairing their ability to remove waste from the bloodstream. This can lead to kidney failure.

The various forms of diabetes

Type 1 diabetes is an autoimmune disease that causes the pancreas' insulin-producing cells to be attacked and destroyed. It is believed that a combination of genetic and environmental factors causes type 1 diabetes.

The symptoms of type 1 diabetes can develop suddenly and can include:

- Increased thirst
- Frequent urination
- Extreme hunger
- Unexplained weight loss
- Fatigue
- Blurred vision
- Slow-healing sores
- Dry, itchy skin

Type 1 diabetes is a lifelong condition, and there is no cure. People with type 1 diabetes need to take insulin every day to manage their blood sugar levels.

Type 2 diabetes is the most common form of diabetes. It occurs when the body becomes resistant to insulin or doesn't produce enough insulin. Type 2 diabetes is thought to be caused by a combination of genetic and lifestyle factors.

The symptoms of type 2 diabetes can develop gradually and may not be noticeable at first. Some common symptoms of type 2 diabetes include:

- Increased thirst
- Frequent urination
- Extreme hunger
- Fatigue
- Blurred vision
- Slow-healing sores
- Dark patches of skin on the neck, armpits, and groin
- Numbness or tingling in the hands and feet

Type 2 diabetes can often be managed with diet and exercise, but some people also need to take medication or insulin.

Gestational diabetes is a type of diabetes that develops during pregnancy. It usually goes away after the baby is born, but it can increase the risk of developing type 2 diabetes later in life.

The symptoms of gestational diabetes are similar to the symptoms of type 2 diabetes. However, many women with gestational diabetes do not have any symptoms.

Gestational diabetes can often be managed with diet and exercise, but some women also need to take medication or insulin.

Prediabetes

Prediabetes is a condition in which blood sugar levels are higher than normal but not high enough to be diagnosed with type 2 diabetes. People with prediabetes are at increased risk of developing type 2 diabetes and other health problems, such as heart disease and stroke.

There are no obvious symptoms of prediabetes. The only way to know if you have prediabetes is to get tested.

If you have prediabetes, there are things you can do to reduce your risk of developing type 2 diabetes, such as:

- Losing weight
- Eating a healthy diet
- Exercising regularly
- Taking medication (if prescribed by your doctor)

If you have any of the risk factors for diabetes, it is important to talk to your doctor about ways to reduce your risk and get tested regularly.

The causes of diabetes

The exact cause of type 1 diabetes is unknown. However, it is thought to be caused by a combination of genetic and environmental factors.

Type 2 diabetes is caused by a combination of genetic and lifestyle factors. Lifestyle factors that can increase the risk of type 2 diabetes include:

- Being overweight or obese
- Having a family history of diabetes
- Being physically inactive
- Eating a healthy diet
- Being older than 45

Gestational diabetes is caused by changes in the way the body metabolizes glucose during pregnancy.

The risk factors for diabetes

The risk factors for type 1 diabetes include:

- Family history of type 1 diabetes
- Certain autoimmune diseases, such as celiac disease and Graves' disease
- Having been born to a mother with type 1 diabetes

- Being Caucasian

The risk factors for type 2 diabetes include:

- Family history of type 2 diabetes
- Being overweight or obese
- Having a sedentary lifestyle
- Eating a healthy diet
- Being older than 45
- Having gestational diabetes
- Having polycystic ovary syndrome (PCOS)
- Having certain medical conditions, such as high blood pressure and high cholesterol

Diabetes is a serious health condition, but it can be managed with proper treatment. If you have any of the risk factors for diabetes, it is important to talk to your doctor about ways to reduce your risk.

THE IMPORTANCE OF DIET
IN MANAGING DIABETES

Let's delve deeper into the strong relationship between diabetes and diet.

How diet affects blood sugar levels

When you eat food, your body breaks it down into glucose, a type of sugar. Glucose enters your bloodstream and is used by your cells for energy. Your pancreas then releases a hormone called insulin, which helps your cells to absorb glucose from the bloodstream.

If you have diabetes, your body either doesn't produce enough insulin or doesn't use insulin properly. This causes glucose to build up in your bloodstream. Over time, high blood sugar levels can damage your nerves, blood vessels, and organs.

Eating a healthy diabetic diet can help to control your blood sugar levels by:

- Reducing the amount of carbohydrates you eat
- Choosing healthy carbohydrates that are low in glycemic index (GI)
- Eating regular meals and snacks throughout the day
- Including protein and fat in your meals and snacks

Glycemic index (GI) is a measure of how quickly a food raises blood sugar levels. Foods with a high GI cause blood sugar levels to rise quickly, while foods with a low GI cause blood sugar levels to rise more slowly.

When you eat a high-GI food, your body releases a lot of insulin to try to bring your blood sugar levels back down. This can lead to a blood sugar spike, followed by a crash. Blood sugar spikes and crashes can make you feel tired, hungry, and irritable.

Eating low-GI foods can help to prevent blood sugar spikes and crashes. Low-GI foods are absorbed into the bloodstream more slowly, so they cause blood sugar levels to rise more gradually.

Here are some examples of high-GI foods:

- White bread
- White rice
- Pasta
- Sugary drinks
- Potatoes
- Corn

Here are some examples of low-GI foods:

- Whole grains
- Fruits
- Vegetables
- Beans
- Lentils
- Nuts

Eating regular meals and snacks throughout the day can also help to control blood sugar levels. This prevents your blood sugar levels from getting too low, which can lead to hypoglycemia (low blood sugar).

Including protein and fat in your meals and snacks can also help to control blood sugar levels. Protein and fat help to slow down the absorption of carbohydrates into the bloodstream. This can help to prevent blood sugar spikes.

How to choose healthy foods and drinks

When choosing foods and drinks for your diabetic diet, it is important to focus on nutrient-rich foods that are low in calories, saturated and unhealthy fats, added sugar, and sodium.

Here are some tips for choosing healthy foods and drinks:

- Choose whole grains over refined grains. Whole grains are a good source of fiber, which can help to slow down the absorption of carbohydrates into the bloodstream.
- Choose lean protein sources, such as fish, chicken, beans, and tofu. Lean protein sources are low in saturated fat and calories. They are also a good source of essential nutrients, such as iron and zinc.
- Limit your intake of saturated and unhealthy fats. Saturated and unhealthy fats can raise cholesterol levels and increase the risk of heart disease. Good sources of healthy fats include olive oil, avocados, and nuts.
- Choose fruits and vegetables over processed foods and sugary drinks. Fruits and vegetables are a good source of vitamins, minerals, and antioxidants. They are also low in calories and saturated fat. Processed foods and sugary drinks are often high in calories, saturated fat, added sugar, and sodium.

- Choose water, unsweetened tea, or coffee over sugary drinks. Sugary drinks are high in calories and added sugar. They can also cause blood sugar levels to rise quickly.

MEAL PLANNING AND PORTION CONTROL

Meal planning and portion control are two of the most important aspects of managing diabetes. By planning your meals ahead of time and eating appropriate portion sizes, you can help to control your blood sugar levels, reduce your risk of complications from diabetes, and improve your overall health.

How to create a healthy meal plan

When creating a healthy meal plan, it is important to consider your individual needs and goals. What foods do you like and dislike? What dietary restrictions do you have? What foods fit into your budget and lifestyle? Once you have considered these factors, you can start to create a plan that is both realistic and effective.

Here are some tips for creating a healthy meal plan for diabetes:

- Make sure your meals and snacks are balanced. Each meal should include a variety of foods from all food groups, including carbohydrates, protein, fat, fruits, and vegetables. This will help you to get the nutrients you need to stay healthy and manage your diabetes.
- Focus on low-glycemic index (GI) carbohydrates. Low-GI carbohydrates are absorbed into the bloodstream more slowly, which helps to prevent blood sugar spikes. Good sources of low-GI carbohydrates include whole grains, fruits, vegetables, and legumes.

- Choose lean protein sources. Lean protein sources are low in saturated fat and calories and high in essential nutrients. Good sources of lean protein include chicken, fish, beans, lentils, tofu, and low-fat dairy products.
- Limit saturated and unhealthy fats. Saturated and unhealthy fats can raise cholesterol levels and increase the risk of heart disease. Good sources of healthy fats include olive oil, avocados, nuts, and seeds.
- Include plenty of fruits and vegetables. Fruits and vegetables are low in calories and fat and high in vitamins, minerals, and antioxidants. They are also a good source of fiber, which can help to slow down the absorption of carbohydrates into the bloodstream.

How to portion your meals and snacks

Portion control is essential for managing diabetes. Eating too much of any food, even healthy foods, can cause your blood sugar levels to rise.

Here are some tips for portioning your meals and snacks:

- Use a food scale or measuring cups and spoons to measure your portions. This will help you to avoid overeating.
- Follow the serving sizes listed on food labels. Serving sizes can help you to understand how much food you should be eating.
- Divide your plate into thirds. Fill one-third of your plate with protein, one-third with carbohydrates, and one-third with vegetables. This will help you to create a balanced meal.
- Avoid eating straight from food containers. This can make it easy to overeat.
- Eat slowly and savor your food. This will help you to feel full and satisfied with your meal.

Tips for eating out

Eating out can be challenging for people with diabetes, but it is possible to make healthy choices.

Here are some tips:

- Choose restaurants with healthy options. Many restaurants now offer healthy menu items, such as grilled or baked dishes, salads, and whole grains. Look for restaurants that have a variety of healthy options to choose from.
- Ask about the ingredients in the food. If you are unsure about the ingredients in a dish, ask the server or chef. They may be able to make modifications to accommodate your needs.
- Beware of hidden sugars and fats. Many restaurant dishes are high in sugar and fat. Be careful of creamy sauces, dressings, and desserts.
- Choose smaller portions. Restaurant portions are often large. Ask for a half portion or share a meal with a friend.
- Avoid sugary drinks. Sugary drinks can add a lot of calories and sugar to your meal. Choose water, unsweetened tea, or coffee instead.

By following these tips, you can create a healthy meal plan, portion your meals and snacks appropriately, and make healthy choices when eating out. This will help you to manage your diabetes and improve your overall health.

DEALING WITH FROM DIABETES

Diabetes is a chronic disease that can lead to a number of serious complications, including heart disease, stroke, and kidney disease. However, there are a number of things that people with diabetes can do to prevent and manage these complications.

Heart disease

Diabetes is a major risk factor for heart disease. People with diabetes are more likely to develop atherosclerosis, a condition in which plaque builds up in the arteries. This can lead to heart attack, stroke, and other cardiovascular problems.

How to prevent heart disease?
There are a number of things that people with diabetes can do to prevent heart disease, including:

- Maintaining a healthy weight

- Eating a healthy diet

- Exercising regularly

- Managing blood sugar levels

- Controlling blood pressure

- Quitting smoking

If you have diabetes and heart disease, there are a number of things you can do to manage your condition, including:

- Taking medications as prescribed by your doctor.

- Making lifestyle changes, such as eating a healthy diet and exercising regularly

- Monitoring your blood sugar levels and blood pressure regularly.

Stroke

Stroke is another serious complication of diabetes. Stroke occurs when the blood supply to the brain is interrupted. This can damage brain tissue and lead to disability or death.

How to prevent stroke?

The same things that help to prevent heart disease also help to prevent stroke. These include:

- Maintaining a healthy weight

- Eating a healthy diet

- Exercising regularly

- Managing blood sugar levels

- Controlling blood pressure

- Quitting smoking

If you have diabetes and have had a stroke, there are a number of things you can do to manage your condition, including:

- Taking medications as prescribed by your doctor.

- Making lifestyle changes, such as eating a healthy diet and exercising regularly

- Monitoring your blood sugar levels and blood pressure regularly.

- Going to rehabilitation therapy to help you regain any lost function.

Kidney disease

Kidney disease is a condition in which the kidneys are damaged and unable to filter waste products from the blood properly. This can lead to a number of serious health problems, including heart disease, stroke, and death.

How to prevent kidney disease?

The best way to prevent kidney disease is to keep blood sugar levels under control. Other things that can help to prevent kidney disease include:

- Maintaining a healthy weight

- Eating a healthy diet

- Exercising regularly

- Controlling blood pressure

- Quitting smoking

Managing kidney disease

If you have diabetes and kidney disease, there are a number of things you can do to manage your condition, including:

- Taking medications as prescribed by your doctor.

- Making lifestyle changes, such as eating a healthy diet and exercising regularly

- Monitoring your blood sugar levels and blood pressure regularly.

- Going to dialysis or having a kidney transplant if necessary

In spite of the fact that diabetes is a significant health risk, it is possible to prevent or delay consequences and learn how to manage cardiovascular disease, stroke, and renal disease if you take the appropriate precautions and pay attention to the information presented in this part.

Here are some additional suggestions for avoiding issues caused by diabetes and treating them:

- Visit your physician for routine examinations and screenings on a regular basis. Early detection and treatment of any issues will be facilitated as a result of this.

- Joining a support group for persons who have diabetes is a good idea. The ability to receive support and guidance from other people who are going through the same thing can be a very beneficial aspect of this.

- Become knowledgeable about diabetes and the difficulties that it can cause. Your ability to manage your condition will improve in proportion to the amount of information you have collected about it.

Do not forget that you are not alone. It is estimated that millions of individuals are living with diabetes, and there are a great deal of tools available to assist you in managing your illness and leading a healthy life.

INSIGHTS INTO THE PATHOLOGY

Exercise and diabetes

Exercise is an important part of diabetes management. It can help to improve blood sugar control, reduce the risk of heart disease and stroke, and improve overall fitness and well-being.

Exercise helps to lower blood sugar levels by:

- Increasing insulin sensitivity: Insulin is a hormone that helps the body to use glucose for energy. Exercise helps to make the body's cells more sensitive to insulin, so that they can use glucose more effectively.
- Reducing glucose production: The liver produces glucose, the main type of sugar in the blood. Exercise helps to reduce the amount of glucose that the liver produces.
- Increasing muscle mass: Muscle tissue uses glucose for energy. Exercise helps to increase muscle mass, which means that the body has more places to store glucose.

How much exercise do you need?

The American Diabetes Association recommends that adults with diabetes get at least 150 minutes of moderate-intensity aerobic activity or 75 minutes of vigorous-intensity aerobic activity each week. They also recommend that adults with diabetes do strength training exercises that work all major muscle groups at least two times per week.

What types of exercise are best?

Any type of exercise that you enjoy and can stick with is good for you. However, some types of exercise are better for people with diabetes than others. Aerobic exercise, such as walking, running, biking, and swimming, is especially beneficial for people with diabetes. Strength training exercises, such as lifting weights or using resistance bands, can also be helpful.

How to get started with exercise

If you are new to exercise, start slowly and gradually increase the amount of time and intensity of your workouts. It is also important to talk to your doctor before starting any new exercise program.

Here are some tips for incorporating exercise into your diabetes management plan:

- Choose activities that you enjoy and that fit into your lifestyle.
- Set realistic goals and start slowly.
- Gradually increase the amount of time and intensity of your workouts.
- Find a workout buddy or join a fitness class to help you stay motivated.
- Listen to your body and take breaks when you need them.

Stress management and diabetes

Stress is an inherent part of daily life, and while it's normal to experience it, excessive stress can pose significant challenges for individuals with diabetes. This is because stress can lead to an increase in blood sugar levels, making the management of diabetes more complex.

Understanding How Stress Affects Blood Sugar Levels

When stress takes hold, the body responds by releasing hormones such as cortisol and adrenaline. These hormones, in response to stress, can elevate blood sugar levels, creating a difficult scenario for those trying to manage their diabetes effectively.

Strategies for Stress Management

Effective stress management is crucial for individuals with diabetes. Here are some practical strategies to combat stress:

- Regular Exercise: Engaging in physical activity on a routine basis is a powerful way to alleviate stress. Exercise triggers the release of endorphins, which are known as "feel-good" hormones.
- Adequate Sleep: Prioritizing quality sleep is essential for overall health, particularly for individuals with diabetes. Lack of sleep can result in elevated blood sugar levels.

- Healthy Diet: A well-balanced diet plays a pivotal role in stress management. Consuming nutritious foods can help stabilize blood sugar levels.
- Relaxation Techniques: Practices like yoga and meditation are effective in reducing stress and promoting a sense of calm.
- Professional Support: Speaking with a therapist or counselor can provide valuable guidance and support in coping with stress.

Additional Lifestyle Factors Impacting Diabetes

Beyond stress management, various other lifestyle factors also influence diabetes management. Here's a look at how sleep, smoking, and alcohol consumption can impact diabetes:

- **Sleep**: Quality sleep is fundamental to overall health. Inadequate sleep can lead to elevated blood sugar levels, making it a concern for individuals with diabetes.
- **Smoking**: Smoking is detrimental to blood vessels and can complicate diabetes management.
- **Alcohol Consumption**: Alcohol has the potential to lower blood sugar levels, which can be risky for those with diabetes.

Incorporating Exercise, Stress Management, and More

Exercise, stress management, and the consideration of lifestyle factors like sleep, smoking, and alcohol consumption all contribute to effective diabetes management. By implementing the recommendations in this chapter, you can learn how to integrate these elements into your diabetes management plan, ultimately improving your overall health and well-being.

CONCLUSION

Diabetes is a chronic disease affecting millions of individuals worldwide. It is a severe disease, but one that can be effectively managed through diet, exercise, and medication.

It is crucial that individuals with diabetes over the age of 50 pay special attention to their diet. Diet can have a significant effect on blood sugar levels, overall health, and quality of life.

This book provides a comprehensive overview of the diabetic diet for individuals over the age of 50. It has covered the fundamentals of meal planning and portion control as well as the most recent research on diabetes and diet. The book also contains a variety of healthy and delectable meal and snack recipes. One of the central themes of this book is that diabetes does not have to rule your existence. People with diabetes can live long, healthy, and fulfilling lives with proper management.

As mentioned in the book, the following are specific measures that persons over 50 with diabetes can take to manage their condition and live healthier lives:

- Consume a diet low in processed foods, sugary beverages, and saturated and unhealthful lipids.
- Concentrate on consuming an abundance of fruits, vegetables, and whole cereals.
- Choose lean sources of protein like fish, fowl, and beans.
- Get consistent exercise. Most days of the week, aim for at least 30 minutes of moderate-intensity exercise.

- Regularly monitor your blood sugar levels. This will allow you to identify any alterations and make any necessary adjustments to your diet, exercise regimen, or medication.
- Develop a personalized diabetes management plan with the help of your clinician.

Diabetes can be difficult to manage, but it is not insurmountable. By following the advice in this book, persons over the age of 50 with diabetes can gain control of their condition and live long, healthy, and fulfilling lives.

Please do not lose faith. Diabetes does not preclude a long, healthy, and fulfilling existence. Listed below are some items that can help you remain optimistic and motivated:

- Concentrate on the things you can influence. You have the ability to manage your diet, exercise regimen, and medication. Also under your control is your demeanor. Choose to be optimistic and optimistic even on difficult days.
- Surround yourself with positive influences. Discuss your diabetes with your family, colleagues, and healthcare team. They can provide you with encouragement and support.
- Find a support group for diabetes. There are numerous support organizations available for diabetics and their families. These associations can foster a sense of community and provide support.
- Commemorate your achievements. Every small measure matters. When you achieve an objective, you should celebrate your accomplishment. This will help you maintain your motivation and focus.

I have faith in you. Diabetes does not preclude a long, healthy, and fulfilling existence.

USEFUL LINK

- ✓ American Diabetes Association https://diabetesjournals.org/
- ✓ National Institute of Diabetes and Digestive and Kidney Diseases (NIDDK) https://www.niddk.nih.gov/
- ✓ Centers for Disease Control and Prevention (CDC) -> https://www.cdc.gov/
- ✓ Joslin Diabetes Center -> https://www.joslin.org/
- ✓ Mayo Clinic -> https://www.mayoclinic.org/
- ✓ WebMD -> https://en.wikipedia.org/wiki/WebMD
- ✓ Diabetes Forecast -> https://www2.diabetes.org/healthy-living
- ✓ Beyond Type 1 -> https://beyondtype1.org/
- ✓ JDRF (Juvenile Diabetes Research Foundation) -> https://www.jdrf.org/
- ✓ DiabetesMine -> https://www.healthline.com/diabetesmine
- ✓ Diabetes Daily -> https://www.diabetesdaily.com/
- ✓ Diabetes News Flash -> https://medicalxpress.com/tags/diabetes/
- ✓ Healthline -> https://www.healthline.com/
- ✓ Medical News Today -> https://www.medicalnewstoday.com/

THE COOKBOOK

BREAKFAST

OVERNIGHT OATS WITH BERRIES AND NUTS

Servings: 1   Prep time: 5 min   Cook time: /

INGREDIENTS

- 1/2 cup rolled oats
- 1/2 cup milk of your choice
- 1/4 cup berries of your choice
- 1 tablespoon nuts of your choice

DIRECTIONS

1.   In a jar or bowl, combine the oats, milk, berries, and nuts.
2.   Stir well, then cover and refrigerate overnight.
3.   In the morning, enjoy your overnight oats!

Cal per 100 g: 120   **Carbs: 15 g**   **Protein: 5 g**   **Fat: 5 g**

AVOCADO TOAST WITH EGGS

Servings: 1   Prep time: 5 min   Cook time: 5 min

INGREDIENTS

- 1 slice whole-wheat bread
- 1/4 avocado, mashed
- 1 egg
- Salt and pepper to taste

DIRECTIONS

1.   Toast the bread and spread the mashed avocado on the toast.
3.   Cook the egg to your liking.
4.   Place the egg on the avocado toast and season with salt and pepper to taste.

Cal per 100 g: 200   **Carbs: 10 g**   **Protein: 12 g**   **Fat: 15 g**

YOGURT WITH FRUIT AND NUTS

Servings: 1   Prep time: 5 min   Cook time: /

INGREDIENTS

- 1 cup plain Greek yogurt
- 1/2 cup berries of your choice
- 1 tablespoon nuts of your choice

DIRECTIONS

1. In a bowl, combine the yogurt, berries, and nuts.
2. Stir well and enjoy!

Cal per 100 g: 150   Carbs: 15 g   Protein: 10 g   Fat: 5 g

WHOLE-WHEAT SMOOTHIE

Servings: 1   Prep time: 5 min   Cook time: /

INGREDIENTS

- 1 cup milk of your choice
- 1/2 cup whole-wheat berries
- 1/4 cup berries of your choice
- 1 tablespoon nuts of your choice
- 1 teaspoon ground cinnamon

DIRECTIONS

1. Combine all ingredients in a blender and blend until smooth.
2. Enjoy!

Cal per 100 g: 120   Carbs: 20 g   Protein: 5 g   Fat: 5 g

CHIA SEED PUDDING WITH FRUIT

Servings: 1   Prep time: 5 min   Cook time: /

INGREDIENTS

- Chia seeds: 2 tablespoons
- Milk: 1/2 cup
- Vanilla extract: 1/2 teaspoon

DIRECTIONS

1. In a bowl, combine the chia seeds, milk, and vanilla extract.
2. Stir well and cover.
3. Refrigerate for at least 30 minutes, or overnight.
4. In the morning, top with your favorite fruit and enjoy!

Cal per 100 g: 100   **Carbs: 15 g**   **Protein: 5 g**   **Fat: 5 g**

EASY DIABETIC-FRIENDLY SCRAMBLED EGGS

Servings: 1   Prep time: 5 min   Cook time: 10 min

INGREDIENTS

- 1 tablespoon olive oil
- 1/4 cup chopped vegetables, such as onions, peppers, and mushrooms
- 2 large eggs
- 1/4 cup milk of your choice
- 1/4 teaspoon salt
- 1/8 teaspoon black pepper

DIRECTIONS

Heat the olive oil in a nonstick skillet over medium heat.
2. Add the vegetables and cook until softened, about 5 minutes.
3. In a bowl, whisk together the eggs, milk, salt, and pepper.
4. Pour the egg mixture into the skillet and cook, stirring constantly, until the eggs are scrambled and cooked through, about 5 minutes.
5. Serve immediately.

Cal per 100 g: 173   **Carbs: 7 g**   **Protein: 15 g**   **Fat: 10 g**

WHOLE-WHEAT PANCAKES WITH BERRIES AND NUTS

Servings: 4   Prep time: 10 min   Cook time: 10 min

INGREDIENTS

- 1 cup whole-wheat flour
- 1 teaspoon baking powder
- 1/4 teaspoon salt
- 1 egg
- 1 cup milk of your choice
- 1/4 cup berries of your choice
- 1 tablespoon nuts of your choice

DIRECTIONS

1. In a bowl, whisk together the flour, baking powder, and salt.
2. In a separate bowl, whisk together the egg and milk.
3. Add the wet ingredients to the dry ingredients and whisk until just combined.
4. Fold in the berries and nuts.
5. Heat a lightly greased griddle or frying pan over medium heat.
6. Pour 1/4 cup of batter onto the griddle for each pancake.
7. Cook for 2-3 minutes per side, or until golden brown.
8. Serve immediately with your favorite toppings, such as maple syrup, honey, or yogurt.

Cal per 100 g: 200   **Carbs: 20 g**   **Protein: 10 g**   **Fat: 5 g**

TOFU SCRAMBLE

Servings: 1   Prep time: 5 min   Cook time: 5 min

INGREDIENTS

- 1/2 block extra firm tofu, crumbled
- 1/4 cup chopped vegetables, such as onions, peppers, and mushrooms
- 1 tablespoon olive oil
- Salt and pepper to taste

DIRECTIONS

1. Heat the olive oil in a skillet over medium heat.
2. Add the tofu and vegetables and cook for 5 minutes, or until the vegetables are softened.
3. Season with salt and pepper to taste.
4. Serve immediately with your favorite toppings, such as whole-wheat toast, avocado, or salsa.

Cal per 100 g: 150   **Carbs: 10 g**   **Protein: 15 g**   **Fat: 5 g**

SMOOTHIE WITH YOGURT AND BERRIES

Servings: 1   Prep time: 5 min   Cook time: / min

INGREDIENTS

- 1 cup plain Greek yogurt
- 1/2 cup berries of your choice
- 1/4 cup milk of your choice
- 1 tablespoon ground flaxseed
- 1 teaspoon vanilla extract

DIRECTIONS

1.   Combine all ingredients in a blender and blend until smooth.

Cal per 100 g: 120   **Carbs: 15 g**   **Protein: 10 g**   **Fat: 5 g**

CHIA SEED PUDDING WITH BERRIES AND NUTS

Servings: 1   Prep time: 5 min   Cook time: /

INGREDIENTS

- 1/4 cup chia seeds
- 1 cup unsweetened milk of your choice
- 1/4 cup berries of your choice
- 1 tablespoon nuts of your choice

DIRECTIONS

1.   In a jar or bowl, combine the chia seeds, milk, berries, and nuts.
2.   Stir well and cover.
3.   Refrigerate overnight.
4.   In the morning, stir well and enjoy!

Cal per 100 g: 100   **Carbs: 15 g**   **Protein: 5 g**   **Fat: 5 g**

SMOOTHIE WITH YOGURT, BERRIES, AND SPINACH

Servings: 1   Prep time: 5 min   Cook time: /

INGREDIENTS

- 1 cup plain Greek yogurt
- 1/2 cup berries of your choice
- 1/4 cup spinach
- 1/4 cup unsweetened almond milk
- 1 teaspoon ground flaxseed

DIRECTIONS

1. Combine all ingredients in a blender and blend until smooth.

Cal per 100 g: 120   **Carbs: 15 g**   **Protein: 10 g**   **Fat: 5 g**

SCRAMBLED EGG BREAKFAST BOWL

Servings: 1   Prep time: 10 min   Cook time: 5 min

INGREDIENTS

- 2 large eggs
- 1/2 cup spinach
- 1/4 cup diced tomatoes
- 1/4 cup diced bell peppers

DIRECTIONS

1. Scramble the eggs and sauté the veggies.
2. Serve together.

Cal per 100 g: 98   **Carbs: 4 g**   **Protein: 8 g**   **Fat: 6 g**

GREEK YOGURT PARFAIT

Servings: 1   **Prep time: 10 min**   **Cook time: /**

INGREDIENTS

- 1/2 cup Greek yogurt (unsweetened)
- 1/4 cup mixed berries
- 1 tbsp chopped nuts

DIRECTIONS

1. Layer ingredients in a glass.

Cal per 100 g: 87   **Carbs: 7 g**   **Protein: 4 g**   **Fat: 4 g**

OATMEAL WITH CINNAMON AND ALMONDS

Servings: 1   **Prep time: 5 min**   **Cook time: 5 min**

INGREDIENTS

- 1/2 cup rolled oats
- 1/2 tsp cinnamon
- 1 tbsp chopped almonds

DIRECTIONS

1. Cook oats with water.
2. Add cinnamon and top with almonds.

Cal per 100 g: 71   **Carbs: 12 g**   **Protein: 2 g**   **Fat: 2 g**

WHOLE WHEAT PANCAKES

Servings: 2   Prep time: 10 min   Cook time: 10 min

INGREDIENTS

·1 cup whole wheat flour

·1/2 tsp baking powder

·1 cup low-fat milk

1 egg

DIRECTIONS

1. Mix ingredients

2. cook pancakes, and serve.

Cal per 100 g: 82   **Carbs: 16 g**   **Protein: 4 g**   **Fat: 4 g**

AVOCADO AND TOMATO TOAST

Servings: 1   Prep time: 5 min   Cook time: /

INGREDIENTS

·1 slice whole grain bread

·1/2 avocado

·1/2 tomato, sliced

DIRECTIONS

1. Toast the bread

2. Spread avocado

3. Top with tomato slices.

Cal per 100 g: 130   **Carbs: 15 g**   **Protein: 2 g**   **Fat: 7 g**

PEANUT BUTTER AND BANANA SMOOTHIE

Servings: 1 | Prep time: 5 min | Cook time: /

INGREDIENTS

- 1 banana
- 2 tbsp peanut butter (sugar-free)

1/2 cup low-fat milk

DIRECTIONS

1. Blend all ingredients until smooth.

Cal per 100 g: 85 | **Carbs: 15 g** | **Protein: 3 g** | **Fat: 2 g**

VEGGIE OMELETTE

Servings: 1 | Prep time: 10 min | Cook time: 5 min

INGREDIENTS

- 2 large eggs
- 1/4 cup diced bell peppers
- 1/4 cup diced onions
- 1/4 cup diced zucchini

DIRECTIONS

1. Beat eggs
2. Cook with veggies and fold in half.

Cal per 100 g: 76 | **Carbs: 3 g** | **Protein: 6 g** | **Fat: 4 g**

COTTAGE CHEESE WITH BERRIES

Servings: 1   Prep time: 10 min   Cook time:/

INGREDIENTS

·1/2 cup low-fat cottage cheese

·1/2 cup mixed berries

DIRECTIONS

1. Serve cottage cheese with mixed berries.

Cal per 100 g: 81   **Carbs: 8 g**   **Protein: 9 g**   **Fat: 1 g**

QUINOA BREAKFAST BOWL

Servings: 1   Prep time: 15 min   Cook time: 15 min

INGREDIENTS

·1/2 cup cooked quinoa

·1/4 cup chopped walnuts

·1/4 cup sliced peaches

·1/2 tsp honey (optional)

DIRECTIONS

1. Mix quinoa, walnuts, and peaches.

2. Drizzle with honey if desired.

Cal per 100 g: 119   **Carbs: 17 g**   **Protein: 3 g**   **Fat: 5g**

SPINACH AND MUSHROOM BREAKFAST QUESADILLA

Servings: 1   Prep time: 10 min   Cook time: 10 min

INGREDIENTS

·2 whole wheat tortillas

·1 cup spinach

·1/2 cup sliced mushrooms

·1/4 cup low-fat shredded cheese

DIRECTIONS

1. Layer ingredients on one tortilla.

2. Top with the second, and cook until cheese melts.

Cal per 100 g: 85   **Carbs: 11 g**   **Protein: 4 g**   **Fat: 3 g**

MAIN MEAL

GRILLED SALMON WITH ROASTED VEGETABLES

Servings: 2   Prep time: 10 min   Cook time: 20 min

INGREDIENTS

- 2 (6-ounce) salmon fillets
- 1 tablespoon olive oil
- Salt and pepper to taste
- 1 cup chopped vegetables, such as broccoli, Brussels sprouts, and carrots

DIRECTIONS

1. Preheat oven to 400 degrees F (200 degrees C).
2. Place salmon fillets on a baking sheet and drizzle with olive oil.
3. Season with salt and pepper to taste.
4. Roast in preheated oven for 15-20 minutes, or until salmon is cooked through.
5. While salmon is roasting, toss vegetables with olive oil and salt and pepper to taste.
6. Roast vegetables for 15-20 minutes, or until tender.
7. Serve salmon and vegetables together and enjoy!

Cal per 100 g: 150   **Carbs: 5 g**   **Protein: 25 g**   **Fat: 5 g**

CHICKEN STIR-FRY WITH BROWN RICE

Servings: 2   Prep time: 10 min   Cook time: 15 min

INGREDIENTS

- 1 pound boneless, skinless chicken breasts, cut into bite-sized pieces
- 1 tablespoon olive oil
- 1/2 cup chopped vegetables, such as onions, peppers, and broccoli
- 1 tablespoon soy sauce
- 1 teaspoon cornstarch
- 1/4 cup water
- 2 cups cooked brown rice

DIRECTIONS

1. Heat olive oil in a large skillet or wok over medium-high heat.
2. Add chicken and cook until browned on all sides.
3. Add vegetables and cook until tender.
4. In a small bowl, whisk together soy sauce, cornstarch, and water.
5. Add the soy sauce mixture to the skillet and cook until thickened, about 1 minute.
6. Serve chicken stir-fry over brown rice and enjoy!

Cal per 100 g: 175   **Carbs: 20 g**   **Protein: 25 g**   **Fat: 5 g**

QUINOA SALAD WITH ROASTED CHICKPEAS AND VEGETABLES

Servings: 4   Prep time: 10 min   Cook time: 30 min

INGREDIENTS

- 1 cup quinoa
- 2 cups water
- 1 (15-ounce) can chickpeas, rinsed and drained
- 1/2 cup chopped vegetables, such as tomatoes, cucumbers, and red onion
- 1/4 cup chopped cilantro
- 2 tablespoons olive oil
- 1 tablespoon lemon juice
- Salt and pepper to taste

DIRECTIONS

1. Cook quinoa according to package directions.
2. Preheat oven to 400 degrees F (200 degrees C).
3. Toss chickpeas with olive oil, salt, and pepper.
4. Spread chickpeas in a single layer on a baking sheet and roast for 20-25 minutes, or until crispy.
5. While chickpeas are roasting, combine quinoa, vegetables, cilantro, olive oil, and lemon juice in a large bowl.
6. Season with salt and pepper to taste.
7. Add roasted chickpeas and stir to combine and serve.

Cal per 100 g: 140   **Carbs: 15 g**   **Protein: 5 g**   **Fat: 5 g**

LENTIL SOUP

Servings: 4   Prep time: 10 min   Cook time: 30 min

INGREDIENTS

- 1 cup lentils
- 2 cups vegetable broth
- 1/2 cup chopped onion
- 1/2 cup chopped carrots
- 1/2 cup chopped celery
- 1/4 teaspoon ground cumin
- 1/4 teaspoon ground turmeric
- Salt and pepper to taste

DIRECTIONS

1. Rinse lentils in a fine mesh strainer.

2. Combine lentils, vegetable broth, onion, carrots, celery, cumin, turmeric, salt, and pepper in a large pot.

3. Bring to a boil over medium-high heat.

4. Reduce heat to low and simmer for 30 minutes, or until lentils are tender.

5. Serve hot and enjoy!

Cal per 100 g: 125   **Carbs: 15 g**   **Protein: 5 g**   **Fat: 5 g**

SHRIMP SCAMPI WITH ZUCCHINI NOODLES

Servings: 2   Prep time: 10 min   Cook time: 15 min

INGREDIENTS

- 1 pound shrimp, peeled and deveined
- 1 tablespoon olive oil
- 1/4 cup chopped garlic
- 1/4 cup chopped fresh parsley
- 1/4 teaspoon red pepper flakes
- 1/4 cup dry white wine
- 1/4 cup lemon juice
- 1 zucchini, spiralized into noodles
- Salt and pepper to taste

DIRECTIONS

1. Heat olive oil in a large skillet over medium heat.
2. Add shrimp and cook until browned on both sides.
3. Add garlic, parsley, and red pepper flakes and cook for 1 minute.
4. Add white wine and lemon juice and cook until sauce has thickened, about 2 minutes.
5. Add zucchini noodles and cook until heated through, about 1 minute.
6. Season with salt and pepper to taste.
7. Serve immediately and enjoy!

Cal per 100 g: 145   **Carbs: 10 g**   **Protein: 25 g**   **Fat: 5 g**

TOFU TACOS WITH MANGO PICO DE GALLO

Servings: 2   Prep time: 10 min   Cook time: 15 min

INGREDIENTS

- 1 block extra firm tofu, pressed and drained
- 1 tablespoon olive oil
- 1/2 teaspoon chili powder
- 1/4 teaspoon cumin
- 1/4 teaspoon salt
- 1/4 teaspoon black pepper
- 6 corn tortillas
- 1/2 cup chopped mango
- 1/4 cup chopped red onion
- 1/4 cup chopped cilantro
- 1 tablespoon lime juice
- Salt and pepper to taste

DIRECTIONS

1. Preheat oven to 400 degrees F (200 degrees C).
2. Cube tofu and toss with olive oil, chili powder, cumin, salt, and pepper.
3. Spread tofu on a baking sheet and bake for 15-20 minutes, or until golden brown and crispy.
4. While tofu is baking, combine mango, red onion, cilantro, and lime juice in a bowl.
5. Season with salt and pepper to taste.
6. To assemble tacos, warm tortillas according to package directions.
7. Fill tortillas with tofu, mango pico de gallo, and your favorite toppings, such as shredded lettuce, chopped tomatoes, and avocado.
8. Serve immediately and enjoy!

Cal per 100 g: 200   **Carbs: 20 g**   **Protein: 15 g**   **Fat: 10 g**

BLACK BEAN BURGERS WITH SWEET POTATO FRIES

Servings: 2   Prep time: 15 min   Cook time: 20 min

INGREDIENTS

- 1 (15-ounce) can black beans, drained and rinsed
- 1/2 cup cooked brown rice
- 1/4 cup chopped onion
- 1/4 cup chopped red bell pepper
- 1/4 cup chopped cilantro
- 1 tablespoon ground cumin
- 1/2 teaspoon chili powder
- 1/4 teaspoon salt
- 1/4 teaspoon black pepper
- 1 (20-ounce) bag sweet potato fries

DIRECTIONS

1. Preheat oven to 400 degrees F (200 degrees C).
2. In a food processor, combine black beans, brown rice, onion, bell pepper, cilantro, cumin, chili powder, salt, and pepper.
3. Pulse until the mixture is well combined and slightly chunky.
4. Form the mixture into 4 patties.
5. Place the patties on a baking sheet and bake for 15-20 minutes, or until cooked through.
6. While patties are baking, bake sweet potato fries according to package directions.
7. Serve patties on buns with your favorite toppings, such as lettuce, tomato, and onion and serve with sweet potato fries.

Cal per 100 g: 225   Carbs: 30 g   Protein: 15 g   Fat: 4 g

CHICKEN AND VEGETABLE STIR-FRY WITH BROWN RICE

Servings: 2   Prep time: 10 min   Cook time: 15 min

INGREDIENTS

- 1 pound boneless, skinless chicken breasts, cut into bite-sized pieces
- 1 tablespoon olive oil
- 1/2 cup chopped vegetables, such as onions, peppers, and broccoli
- 1 tablespoon soy sauce
- 1 teaspoon cornstarch
- 1/4 cup water
- 2 cups cooked brown rice

DIRECTIONS

1. Heat olive oil in a large skillet or wok over medium-high heat.
2. Add chicken and cook until browned on all sides.
3. Add vegetables and cook until tender.
4. In a small bowl, whisk together soy sauce, cornstarch, and water.
5. Add the soy sauce mixture to the skillet and cook until thickened, about 1 minute.
6. Serve chicken and vegetable stir-fry over brown rice and enjoy!

Cal per 100 g: 175   Carbs: 20 g   Protein: 25 g   Fat: 5 g

SALMON WITH ROASTED VEGETABLES

Servings: 2   Prep time: 10 min   Cook time: 20 min

INGREDIENTS

INGREDIENTS

- 2 (6-ounce) salmon fillets
- 1 tablespoon olive oil
- Salt and pepper to taste
- 1 cup chopped vegetables, such as broccoli, Brussels sprouts, and carrots

DIRECTIONS

1. Preheat oven to 400 degrees F (200 degrees C).
2. Place salmon fillets on a baking sheet and drizzle with olive oil.
3. Season with salt and pepper to taste.
4. Roast in preheated oven for 15-20 minutes, or until salmon is cooked through.
5. While salmon is roasting, toss vegetables with olive oil and salt and pepper to taste.
6. Roast vegetables for 15-20 minutes, or until tender.
7. Serve salmon and vegetables together and enjoy!

Cal per 100 g: 150   Carbs: 5 g   Protein: 25 g   Fat: 5 g

TOFU SCRAMBLE WITH WHOLE-WHEAT TOAST

Servings: 1   Prep time: 5 min   Cook time: 5 min

INGREDIENTS

- 1/2 block extra firm tofu, crumbled
- 1 tablespoon olive oil
- 1/4 cup chopped vegetables, such as onions, peppers, and mushrooms
- 1/4 teaspoon turmeric powder
- 1/4 teaspoon salt
- 1/4 teaspoon black pepper
- 1 slice whole-wheat toast

DIRECTIONS

1. Heat olive oil in a skillet over medium heat.
2. Add tofu and vegetables and cook until tender, about 5 minutes.
3. Season with turmeric powder, salt, and pepper to taste.
4. Serve tofu scramble on whole-wheat toast and enjoy!

Cal per 100 g: 150   Carbs: 10 g   Protein: 15 g   Fat: 5 g

GRILLED LEMON HERB CHICKEN

Servings: 2   Prep time: 15 min   Cook time: 15 min

INGREDIENTS

- 2 boneless, skinless chicken breasts
- 1 lemon, juiced
- 1 tsp dried herbs (thyme, rosemary, oregano)

DIRECTIONS

1. Marinate chicken in lemon juice and herbs
2. Grill until cooked through.

Cal per 100 g: 110   **Carbs: 2 g**   **Protein: 20 g**   **Fat: 2 g**

ZUCCHINI NOODLES WITH PESTO

Servings: 2   Prep time: 10 min   Cook time: 5 min

INGREDIENTS

- 2 medium zucchinis, spiralized
- 1/4 cup homemade or store-bought pesto (sugar-free)
- 1/4 cup cherry tomatoes, halved

DIRECTIONS

1. Sauté zucchini noodles
2. Mix with pesto
3. Top with cherry tomatoes.

Cal per 100 g: 77   **Carbs: 4 g**   **Protein: 2 g**   **Fat: 7 g**

BAKED SWEET POTATO AND BLACK BEAN TACOS

| Servings: 4 | Prep time: 10 min | Cook time: 30 min |

INGREDIENTS

·4 small sweet potatoes
·1 can (15 oz) black beans, drained and rinsed
·1 tsp chili powder
·1/2 cup salsa (sugar-free)

DIRECTIONS

1. Roast sweet potatoes.
2. Mix black beans with chili powder.
3. Serve as taco filling with salsa.

Cal per 100 g: 95   **Carbs: 20 g**   **Protein: 2 g**   **Fat: 1 g**

LEMON GARLIC SHRIMP WITH BROWN RICE

| Servings: 2 | Prep time: 15 min | Cook time: 15 min |

INGREDIENTS

·1/2 lb large shrimp, peeled and deveined
·1 cup cooked brown rice
·2 cloves garlic, minced
·1 lemon, juiced
·1 tbsp olive oil

DIRECTIONS

1. Sauté shrimp with garlic, lemon juice, and serve over brown rice.

Cal per 100 g: 128   **Carbs: 15 g**   **Protein: 11 g**   **Fat: 3 g**

CHICKEN AND VEGETABLE SKEWERS

Servings: 4   Prep time: 10 min   Cook time: 15 min

INGREDIENTS

·1 lb chicken breast, cut into chunks

·Assorted vegetables (bell peppers, onions, zucchini)

·2 tbsp olive oil

·1 tsp Italian seasoning

DIRECTIONS

1. Thread chicken and vegetables onto skewers
2. brush with olive oil and seasoning
3. grill until cooked

Cal per 100 g: 112   **Carbs: 4 g**   **Protein: 18 g**   **Fat: 4 g**

LENTIL AND VEGETABLE SOUP

Servings: 4   Prep time: 10 min   Cook time: 30 min

INGREDIENTS

·1 cup dried green or brown lentils

·4 cups low-sodium vegetable broth

·1 cup mixed vegetables (carrots, celery, onions)

·2 cloves garlic, minced

·1 tsp cumin

DIRECTIONS

1. Cook lentils and vegetables in broth with cumin until tender

Cal per 100 g: 75   **Carbs: 13 g**   **Protein: 4 g**   **Fat: 1 g**

BAKED CHICKEN AND VEGETABLE FOIL PACKETS

Servings: 2   Prep time: 15 min   Cook time: 25 min

INGREDIENTS

·2 chicken breasts

·2 cups mixed vegetables (broccoli, carrots, bell peppers)

·2 tbsp olive oil

·1 tsp Italian seasoning

DIRECTIONS

1. Season chicken and vegetables
2. wrap in foil
3. bake until chicken is cooked through

Cal per 100 g: 117   **Carbs: 6 g**   **Protein: 18 g**   **Fat: 4 g**

GRILLED CHICKEN AND VEGETABLE SKEWERS

Servings: 4   Prep time: 10 min   Cook time: 15 min

INGREDIENTS

·1 lb boneless, skinless chicken breast, cut into chunks

·Assorted vegetables (bell peppers, zucchini, cherry tomatoes)

·2 tbsp olive oil

·1 tsp Italian seasoning

DIRECTIONS

1. Thread chicken and vegetables onto skewers
2. Brush with olive oil and seasoning
3. Grill until chicken is cooked

Cal per 100 g: 120   **Carbs: 3 g**   **Protein: 19 g**   **Fat: 4 g**

BAKED SALMON WITH LEMON AND DILL

Servings: 2   Prep time: 10 min   Cook time: 20 min

INGREDIENTS

·2 salmon fillets

·1 lemon, sliced

·2 tsp fresh dill

·Salt and pepper to taste

DIRECTIONS

1. Place salmon on a baking sheet

2. Top with lemon slices and dill

3. Bake until salmon flakes easily

Cal per 100 g: 206   **Carbs: 0 g**   **Protein: 22 g**   **Fat: 13 g**

TURKEY AND VEGETABLE STIR-FRY

Servings: 2   Prep time: 15 min   Cook time: 15 min

INGREDIENTS

·1/2 lb ground turkey

·2 cups mixed vegetables (broccoli, bell peppers, snap peas)

·2 cloves garlic, minced

·2 tbsp low-sodium soy sauce

·1 tbsp olive oil

DIRECTIONS

1. Sauté ground turkey, vegetables, and garlic in olive oil. Add soy sauce.

Cal per 100 g: 125   **Carbs: 5 g**   **Protein: 14 g**   **Fat: 6 g**

QUINOA AND BLACK BEAN BOWL

Servings: 4   Prep time: 15 min   Cook time: 15 min

INGREDIENTS

·1 cup quinoa, cooked

·1 can (15 oz) black beans, drained and rinsed

·1 cup cherry tomatoes, halved

·1/4 cup red onion, diced

·1/4 cup fresh cilantro, chopped

·2 tbsp olive oil

·2 tbsp balsamic vinegar

DIRECTIONS

1. Mix all ingredients in a large bowl

2. Drizzle with olive oil and balsamic vinegar.

Cal per 100 g: 130   **Carbs: 21 g**   **Protein: 5 g**   **Fat: 3 g**

GRILLED VEGETABLE QUINOA SALAD

Servings: 4   Prep time: 20 min   Cook time: 10 min

INGREDIENTS

·1 cup quinoa, cooked

·Assorted grilled vegetables

(zucchini, eggplant, bell peppers)

·2 tbsp olive oil

·2 tbsp balsamic vinegar

DIRECTIONS

1. Toss grilled vegetables and quinoa with olive oil and balsamic vinegar

Cal per 100 g: 112   **Carbs: 20 g**   **Protein: 3 g**   **Fat: 4 g**

LEMON GARLIC SHRIMP WITH ASPARAGUS

Servings: 2   Prep time: 10 min   Cook time: 15 min

INGREDIENTS

·1/2 lb large shrimp, peeled and deveined

·1 lb asparagus, trimmed

·2 cloves garlic, minced

·1 lemon, juiced

·2 tbsp olive oil

DIRECTIONS

1. Sauté shrimp and asparagus in olive oil with garlic
2. Finish with lemon juice

Cal per 100 g: 120   Carbs: 4 g   Protein: 14 g   Fat: 7 g

QUINOA STUFFED BELL PEPPERS

Servings: 4   Prep time: 10 min   Cook time: 40 min

INGREDIENTS

·4 large bell peppers

·1 cup quinoa, cooked

·1 lb ground turkey

·1 cup diced tomatoes

·1/2 cup low-sodium chicken broth

DIRECTIONS

1. Brown turkey
2. Mix with quinoa
3. Diced tomatoes and stuff peppers
4. Bake with broth

Cal per 100 g: 121   Carbs: 14 g   Protein: 10 g   Fat: 3 g

GREEK SALAD WITH GRILLED CHICKEN

Servings: 2   Prep time: 10 min   Cook time: 15 min

INGREDIENTS

·2 boneless, skinless chicken breasts

·2 cups mixed greens

·1 cucumber, sliced

·1/2 cup cherry tomatoes, halved

·1/4 cup feta cheese

·2 tbsp Greek dressing (sugar-free)

DIRECTIONS

1. Grill chicken, slice, and serve over a salad of mixed greens, cucumbers, tomatoes, feta cheese, and dressing

Cal per 100 g: 69   Carbs: 4 g   Protein: 9 g   Fat: 2 g

AULIFLOWER RICE STIR-FRY

Servings: 4   Prep time: 10 min   Cook time: 15 min

INGREDIENTS

·1 head cauliflower, grated into "rice"

·2 cups mixed vegetables (broccoli, carrots, bell peppers)

·2 cloves garlic, minced

·2 tbsp low-sodium soy sauce

·1 tbsp sesame oil

DIRECTIONS

1. Sauté cauliflower rice, vegetables, and garlic in sesame oil with soy sauce

Cal per 100 g: 25   Carbs: 5 g   Protein: 1 g   Fat: 1 g

LENTIL SOUP WITH SPINACH

Servings: 4　　　Prep time: 10 min　　　Cook time: 30 min

INGREDIENTS

- 1 cup dried green lentils
- 4 cups low-sodium vegetable broth
- 2 cups fresh spinach
- 1 onion, chopped
- 2 cloves garlic, minced
- 1 tsp cumin

DIRECTIONS

1. In a large pot, sauté the chopped onion and minced garlic in a little olive oil until they become translucent
2. Add the dried lentils to the pot and stir for a couple of minutes
3. Pour in the vegetable broth and bring to a boil
4. Reduce the heat to a simmer, cover, and cook for about 20-25 minutes or until the lentils are tender
5. Stir in the cumin and fresh spinach and continue to cook until the spinach wilts and the flavors meld together
6. Season with salt and pepper to taste

Cal per 100 g: 72　　　Carbs: 13 g　　　Protein: 6 g　　　Fat: 1 g

TURKEY AND QUINOA CHILI

Servings: 4　　　Prep time: 10 min　　　Cook time: 30 min

INGREDIENTS

- 1 pound ground turkey
- 1 onion, chopped
- 2 cloves garlic, minced
- 1 (15-ounce) can black beans, rinsed and drained
- 1 (15-ounce) can kidney beans, rinsed and drained
- 1 (14.5-ounce) can diced tomatoes, undrained
- 1 (10-ounce) package frozen corn
- 1 cup quinoa, cooked
- 1 teaspoon chili powder
- 1/2 teaspoon cumin
- 1/4 teaspoon salt
- 1/4 teaspoon black pepper

DIRECTIONS

1. Brown the ground turkey in a large pot over medium-high heat.
2. Add the onion and garlic and cook until softened, about 5 minutes.
3. Drain off any excess grease.
4. Add the black beans, kidney beans, diced tomatoes, corn, quinoa, chili powder, cumin, salt, and pepper to the pot.
5. Bring to a boil, then reduce heat to low and simmer for 20 minutes, or until the chili has thickened.
6. Serve hot and enjoy!

Cal per 100 g: 125　　　Carbs: 15 g　　　Protein: 10 g　　　Fat: 5 g

SALMON BURGERS WITH SWEET POTATO WEDGES

Servings: 4   **Prep time: 10 min**   **Cook time: 20 min**

INGREDIENTS

- 1 pound salmon fillet, skin removed and bones removed
- 1/4 cup chopped onion
- 1/4 cup chopped cilantro
- 1 tablespoon olive oil
- 1/2 teaspoon salt
- 1/4 teaspoon black pepper
- 1 sweet potato, peeled and cut into wedges
- 1 tablespoon olive oil
- 1/4 teaspoon salt
- 1/4 teaspoon black pepper

DIRECTIONS

1. Preheat oven to 400 degrees F (200 degrees C).
2. In a food processor, combine the salmon, onion, cilantro, olive oil, salt, and pepper.
3. Pulse until the mixture is well combined.
4. Form the mixture into 4 patties.
5. Place the patties on a baking sheet lined with parchment paper.
6. In a separate bowl, combine the sweet potato wedges, olive oil, salt, and pepper.
7. Toss to coat.
8. Spread the sweet potato wedges on a baking sheet.
9. Bake the salmon burgers and sweet potato wedges for 20 minutes, or until cooked through.
10. Serve immediately and enjoy!

Cal per 100 g: 200   **Carbs: 20 g**   **Protein: 20 g**   **Fat: 10 g**

CHICKEN AND BROCCOLI STIR-FRY WITH BROWN RICE

Servings: 4   **Prep time: 10 min**   **Cook time: 15 min**

INGREDIENTS

- 1 pound boneless, skinless chicken breasts, cut into bite-sized pieces
- 1 tablespoon olive oil
- 1/2 cup chopped onion
- 1 cup chopped broccoli florets
- 1/4 cup chopped carrots
- 1 tablespoon soy sauce
- 1 teaspoon cornstarch
- 1/4 cup water
- 2 cups cooked brown rice

DIRECTIONS

1. Heat olive oil in a large skillet or wok over medium-high heat.
2. Add chicken and cook until browned on all sides.
3. Add onion, broccoli, and carrots and cook until tender, about 5 minutes.
4. In a small bowl, whisk together soy sauce, cornstarch, and water.
5. Add the soy sauce mixture to the skillet and cook until thickened, about 1 minute.
6. Serve chicken and broccoli stir-fry over brown rice and enjoy!

Cal per 100 g: 175   **Carbs: 20 g**   **Protein: 25 g**   **Fat: 5 g**

SIDE DISH

ROASTED GARLIC PARMESAN ASPARAGUS

Servings: 4   Prep time: 10 min   Cook time: 15 min

INGREDIENTS

·1 lb fresh asparagus spears

·2 cloves garlic, minced

·2 tbsp olive oil

·2 tbsp grated Parmesan cheese

DIRECTIONS

1. Toss asparagus with olive oil and garlic

2. Roast in the oven and sprinkle with Parmesan before serving.

Cal per 100 g: 32   Carbs: 4 g   Protein: 2 g   Fat: 2 g

CUCUMBER TOMATO SALAD

Servings: 4   Prep time: 10 min   Cook time: /

INGREDIENTS

·2 cucumbers, sliced

·2 tomatoes, diced

·1/4 cup red onion, finely chopped

·2 tbsp fresh basil, chopped

·2 tbsp olive oil

DIRECTIONS

1. Combine cucumbers, tomatoes, red onion, and basil

2. Drizzle with olive oil and toss

Cal per 100 g: 25   Carbs: 3 g   Protein: 1 g   Fat: 2 g

GRILLED ZUCCHINI WITH LEMON AND HERBS

Servings: 4   **Prep time: 10 min**   **Cook time: 10 min**

INGREDIENTS

·4 medium zucchinis, sliced lengthwise

·Zest and juice of 1 lemon

·2 tbsp fresh herbs (such as rosemary or thyme), chopped

·2 tbsp olive oil

DIRECTIONS

1. Brush zucchini with olive oil

2. Grill until tender

3. Sprinkle with lemon zest, juice, and fresh herbs

Cal per 100 g: 17   **Carbs: 3 g**   **Protein: 1 g**   **Fat: 1 g**

QUINOA AND BLACK BEAN SALAD

Servings: 4   **Prep time: 15 min**   **Cook time: 15 min**

INGREDIENTS

·1 cup cooked quinoa

·1 can (15 oz) black beans, drained and rinsed

·1 cup cherry tomatoes, halved

·1/4 cup red onion, diced

·1/4 cup fresh cilantro, chopped

·2 tbsp olive oil

·2 tbsp balsamic vinegar

DIRECTIONS

1. Mix all ingredients in a large bowl

2. Drizzle with olive oil and balsamic vinegar

Cal per 100 g: 129   **Carbs: 21 g**   **Protein: 5 g**   **Fat: 3 g**

SPINACH AND STRAWBERRY SALAD

Servings: 4   Prep time: 10 min   Cook time: /

INGREDIENTS

·8 cups fresh spinach

·1 1/2 cups sliced strawberries

·1/4 cup chopped walnuts

·2 tbsp balsamic vinaigrette (sugar-free)

DIRECTIONS

1. Toss spinach, strawberries, and walnuts with balsamic vinaigrette

Cal per 100 g: 16   **Carbs: 3 g**   **Protein: 1 g**   **Fat: 1 g**

ROASTED BRUSSELS SPROUTS

Servings: 4   Prep time: 10 min   Cook time: 30 min

INGREDIENTS

·1 lb Brussels sprouts, trimmed and halved

·2 tbsp olive oil

·Salt and pepper to taste

·2 tbsp balsamic vinegar (reduced-sugar)

DIRECTIONS

1. Toss Brussels sprouts with olive oil, salt, and pepper
2. Roast until crispy
3. Drizzle with balsamic vinegar

Cal per 100 g: 43   **Carbs: 7 g**   **Protein: 2 g**   **Fat: 2 g**

GREEK CUCUMBER SALAD

Servings: 4   Prep time: 10 min   Cook time: /

INGREDIENTS

·3 cucumbers, sliced

·1/2 cup red onion, thinly sliced

·1/2 cup feta cheese, crumbled

·1/4 cup Kalamata olives, pitted and sliced

·2 tbsp fresh dill, chopped

·2 tbsp olive oil

DIRECTIONS

1. Combine cucumbers, red onion, feta cheese, olives, and dill
2. Drizzle with olive oil and toss

Cal per 100 g: 74   **Carbs: 5 g**   **Protein: 2 g**   **Fat: 5 g**

BROCCOLI WITH GARLIC AND ALMONDS

Servings: 4   Prep time: 10 min   Cook time: 10 min

INGREDIENTS

·1 lb broccoli florets

·2 cloves garlic, minced

·2 tbsp sliced almonds

·2 tbsp olive oil

DIRECTIONS

1. Steam or blanch broccoli until tender-crisp
2. Sauté with garlic and top with almonds

Cal per 100 g: 43   **Carbs: 5 g**   **Protein: 3 g**   **Fat: 3 g**

LEMON-DILL GREEN BEANS

Servings: 4   **Prep time: 10 min**   **Cook time: 10 min**

INGREDIENTS

·1 lb fresh green beans, trimmed

·Zest and juice of 1 lemon

·2 tbsp fresh dill, chopped

·2 tbsp olive oil

DIRECTIONS

1. Steam or blanch green beans until tender-crisp
2. Toss with lemon zest, lemon juice, dill, and olive oil

Cal per 100 g: 25   **Carbs: 4 g**   **Protein: 1 g**   **Fat: 1 g**

CAPRESE SALAD

Servings: 4   **Prep time: 10 min**   **Cook time: /**

INGREDIENTS

·4 ripe tomatoes, sliced

·1 cup fresh mozzarella cheese, sliced

·1/4 cup fresh basil leaves

·2 tbsp extra-virgin olive oil

·Balsamic glaze (sugar-free) for drizzling (optional)

DIRECTIONS

1. Arrange tomato and mozzarella slices on a plate.
2. Tuck basil leaves between the tomato and mozzarella slices.
3. Drizzle with extra-virgin olive oil.
4. Optionally, you can enhance the flavor by adding a sugar-free balsamic glaze drizzle.

Cal per 100 g: 194   **Carbs: 3 g**   **Protein: 9 g**   **Fat: 16 g**

ROASTED BRUSSELS SPROUTS

Servings: 4   Prep time: 10 min   Cook time: 20 min

INGREDIENTS

·1 pound Brussels sprouts, trimmed and halved

·1 tablespoon olive oil

·1/2 teaspoon salt

·1/4 teaspoon black pepper

DIRECTIONS

1. Preheat oven to 400 degrees F (200 degrees C).
2. Toss Brussels sprouts with olive oil, salt, and pepper.
3. Spread Brussels sprouts in a single layer on a baking sheet.
4. Roast for 20 minutes, or until tender and golden brown.
5. Serve immediately and enjoy!

Cal per 100 g: 45   **Carbs: 9 g**   **Protein: 3 g**   **Fat: 2 g**

STEAMED BROCCOLI

Servings: 2   Prep time: 5 min   Cook time: 10 min

INGREDIENTS

·1 head broccoli, cut into florets

DIRECTIONS

1. Fill a steamer pot with water and bring to a boil.
2. Add broccoli florets to the steamer and cook for 5-10 minutes, or until tender.
3. Serve immediately and enjoy!

Cal per 100 g: 35   **Carbs: 6 g**   **Protein: 3 g**   **Fat: 1 g**

ROASTED SWEET POTATOES

Servings: 4   Prep time: 10 min   Cook time: 30 min

INGREDIENTS

· 1 pound sweet potatoes, peeled and cut into cubes
· 1 tablespoon olive oil
· 1/2 teaspoon salt
· 1/4 teaspoon black pepper

DIRECTIONS

1. Preheat oven to 400 degrees F (200 degrees C).
2. Toss sweet potatoes with olive oil, salt, and pepper.
3. Spread sweet potatoes in a single layer on a baking sheet.
4. Roast for 25 minutes, or until tender and golden brown.
5. Serve immediately and enjoy!

Cal per 100 g: 85   Carbs: 20 g   Protein: 2 g   Fat: 1 g

GREEN SALAD WITH OLIVE OIL

Servings: 4   Prep time: 10 min   Cook time: /

INGREDIENTS

· 4 cups mixed greens
· 1/4 cup olive oil
· 2 tablespoons vinegar (such as balsamic, red wine, or apple cider vinegar)
· Salt and pepper to taste

DIRECTIONS

1. In a large bowl, combine mixed greens, olive oil, vinegar, salt, and pepper.
2. Toss to coat.
3. Serve immediately and enjoy!

Cal per 100 g: 45   Carbs: 3 g   Protein: 1 g   Fat: 4 g

TOMATO SALAD WITH BASIL

Servings: 4   Prep time: 10 min   Cook time: /

INGREDIENTS

- 2 pounds tomatoes, sliced
- 1/4 cup chopped fresh basil
- 1 tablespoon olive oil
- 1 teaspoon balsamic vinegar
- Salt and pepper to taste

DIRECTIONS

1. In a large bowl, combine tomatoes, basil, olive oil, balsamic vinegar, salt, and pepper.
2. Toss to coat.
3. Serve immediately and enjoy!

Cal per 100 g: 25   **Carbs: 5 g**   **Protein: 1 g**   **Fat: 1 g**

LENTIL SALAD

Servings: 4   Prep time: 15 min   Cook time: 20 min

INGREDIENTS

- 1 cup lentils
- 1/2 cups vegetable broth
- 1/4 cup chopped onion
- 1/2 cup chopped celery
- 1/2 cup chopped carrots
- 1/4 cup chopped fresh parsley
- 1 tablespoon olive oil
- 1/2 tablespoon lemon juice
- Salt and pepper to taste

DIRECTIONS

1. Cook lentils according to package directions.
2. While lentils are cooking, combine onion, celery, carrots, and parsley in a large bowl.
3. Drain lentils and add them to the bowl with the vegetables.
4. Add olive oil, lemon juice, salt, and pepper.
5. Toss to coat.
6. Serve immediately and enjoy!

Cal per 100 g: 90   **Carbs: 15 g**   **Protein: 8 g**   **Fat: 4 g**

QUINOA SALAD WITH ROASTED VEGETABLES

Servings: 4   Prep time: 10 min   Cook time: 30 min

INGREDIENTS

- 1 cup quinoa
- 2 cups vegetable broth
- 1 cup roasted vegetables (such as broccoli, Brussels sprouts, or sweet potatoes)
- 1/2 cup chopped onion
- 1/4 cup chopped fresh parsley
- 2 tablespoons olive oil
- 1 tablespoon lemon juice
- Salt and pepper to taste

DIRECTIONS

1. Cook quinoa according to package directions.
2. While quinoa is cooking, roast vegetables according to package directions.
3. In a large bowl, combine quinoa, roasted vegetables, onion, parsley, olive oil, lemon juice, salt, and pepper.
4. Toss to coat.
5. Serve immediately and enjoy!

Cal per 100 g: 135   **Carbs: 20 g**   **Protein: 5 g**   **Fat: 5 g**

COLESLAW WITH GREEK YOGURT DRESSING

Servings: 4   Prep time: 10 min   Cook time: /

INGREDIENTS

- 4 cups shredded cabbage
- 1/2 cup shredded carrots
- 1/4 cup chopped onion
- 1/4 cup Greek yogurt
- 1 tablespoon lemon juice
- 1 teaspoon Dijon mustard
- Salt and pepper to taste

DIRECTIONS

1. In a large bowl, combine cabbage, carrots, and onion.
2. In a separate bowl, whisk together Greek yogurt, lemon juice, Dijon mustard, salt, and pepper.
3. Pour dressing over cabbage mixture and toss to coat.
4. Serve immediately and enjoy!

Cal per 100 g: 55   **Carbs: 7 g**   **Protein: 3 g**   **Fat: 3 g**

ARTICHOKE SALAD

Servings: 4   Prep time: 15 min   Cook time: /

INGREDIENTS

·1 can (14 ounces) artichoke hearts, drained and quartered

·1/2 cup chopped red onion

·1/4 cup crumbled feta cheese

·2 tablespoons olive oil

·2 tablespoons lemon juice

·Salt and pepper to taste

DIRECTIONS

1. In a large bowl, combine artichoke hearts, onion, feta cheese, olive oil, lemon juice, salt, and pepper

2. Toss to coat

3. Serve immediately and enjoy!

Cal per 100 g: 110   **Carbs: 10 g**   **Protein: 5 g**   **Fat: 8 g**

PUERTO RICAN TOSTONES (FRIED PLANTAINS)

Servings: 2   Prep time: 10 min   Cook time: 10 min

INGREDIENTS

·1 green plantain

·5 tablespoons oil for frying

·3 cups cold water

DIRECTIONS

1. Peel plantain and cut into 1-inch slices. Fill a bowl with 3 cups of cold water.

2. Heat oil in a large deep skillet over medium-high heat; add plantain slices in an even layer and fry on both sides until golden brown, about 3 1/2 minutes per side. Set skillet aside.

3. Transfer plantain slices to a chopping board; flatten each one by placing a small plate on top and pressing down. Dip plantain slices in cold water.

4. Reheat oil in the skillet over medium heat; cook plantain slices for 1 minute on each side. Season to taste with salt and serve immediately.

Cal per serv.: 136   **Carbs: 29 g**   **Protein: 1 g**   **Fat: 3 g**

SUPERFAST ASPARAGUS

Servings: 3   Prep time: 10 min   Cook time: 10 min

INGREDIENTS

·1 pound asparagus

·1 teaspoon Cajun seasoning

DIRECTIONS

1. Preheat oven to 425 degrees F (220 degrees C).

2. Snap the asparagus at the tender part of the stalk. Arrange spears in one layer on a baking sheet. Spray lightly with nonstick spray; sprinkle with the Cajun seasoning.

3. Bake in the preheated oven until tender, about 10 minutes.

Cal per 100 g: 110   Carbs: 10 g   Protein: 5 g   Fat: 6 g

SPICY BAKED SWEET POTATO FRIES

Servings: 6   Prep time: 10 min   Cook time: 60 min

INGREDIENTS

·6 sweet potatoes, cut into French fries

·2 tablespoons canola oil

·3 tablespoons taco seasoning mix

·¼ teaspoon cayenne pepper

DIRECTIONS

1. Preheat the oven to 425 degrees F (220 degrees C).

2. In a plastic bag, combine the sweet potatoes, canola oil, taco seasoning, and cayenne pepper. Close and shake the bag until the fries are evenly coated. Spread the fries out in a single layer on two large baking sheets.

3. Bake for 30 minutes, or until crispy and brown on one side. Turn the fries over using a spatula, and cook for another 30 minutes, or until they are all crispy on the outside and tender inside. Thinner fries may not take as long.

Cal per 100 g: 110   Carbs: 10 g   Protein: 5 g   Fat: 5 g

BEVERAGE

CUCUMBER AND MINT INFUSED WATER

Servings: 1   Prep time: 5 min

INGREDIENTS

·1/2 cucumber, sliced

·4-5 fresh mint leaves

·1 cup of water

DIRECTIONS

1. Place cucumber slices and mint leaves in a glass of water
2. Let it infuse for a refreshing and hydrating drink

GREEN TEA WITH LEMON

Servings: 1   Prep time: 5 min

INGREDIENTS

·1 green tea bag

·1 slice of lemon

·1 cup of hot water

DIRECTIONS

1. Steep the green tea bag in hot water and add a slice of lemon for a refreshing and antioxidant-rich beverage

CINNAMON APPLE SPICE TEA

Servings: 1   Prep time: 5 min

INGREDIENTS

·1 apple spice herbal tea bag

·1/2 tsp ground cinnamon

·1 cup of hot water

DIRECTIONS

1. Steep the apple spice herbal tea bag in hot water
2. Add ground cinnamon for extra flavor, and enjoy this warm and comforting beverage

ICED COFFEE WITH ALMOND MILK

Servings: 1   Prep time: 5 min

INGREDIENTS

·1/2 cup unsweetened iced coffee

·1/2 cup unsweetened almond milk

·Ice cubes

DIRECTIONS

1. Mix iced coffee and almond milk
2. Add ice cubes and you have a refreshing iced coffee.

SPARKLING WATER WITH LIME

Servings: 1   Prep time: 2 min

INGREDIENTS

·Sparkling water
·1-2 slices of fresh lime

DIRECTIONS

1. Add slices of fresh lime to sparkling water for a zesty and hydrating beverage

GINGER AND TURMERIC TEA

Servings: 1   Prep time: 10 min

INGREDIENTS

·1 ginger tea bag
·1/2 tsp ground turmeric
·1 cup of hot water

DIRECTIONS

1. Steep the ginger tea bag in hot water and add ground turmeric for a soothing and anti-inflammatory tea

BLUEBERRY AND SPINACH SMOOTHIE

Servings: 1   Prep time: 5 min

INGREDIENTS

·1/2 cup frozen blueberries
·1 cup fresh spinach
·1/2 cup unsweetened almond milk

DIRECTIONS

1. Blend the blueberries, spinach, and almond milk for a nutrient-packed, low-carb smoothie

CHIA SEED AND LEMON WATER

Servings: 1   Prep time: 5 min

INGREDIENTS

·1 tbsp chia seeds
·1/2 lemon, juiced
·1 cup of water

DIRECTIONS

1. Mix chia seeds, lemon juice, and water
2. Let it sit for a while to create a refreshing and fiber-rich beverage

CINNAMON AND ALMOND MILK LATTE

Servings: 1   Prep time: 2 min

INGREDIENTS

·1/2 tsp ground cinnamon
·1 cup unsweetened almond milk

DIRECTIONS

1. Heat almond milk and add ground cinnamon for a warm and comforting latte with a hint of spice

UNSWEETENED ICED TEA

Servings: 1   Prep time: 10 min

INGREDIENTS

·1 cup brewed unsweetened tea
·1/2 cup ice

DIRECTIONS

1. Combine brewed tea and ice in a glass
2. Stir to combine
3. Serve immediately and enjoy!

SPARKLING WATER WITH LEMON

Servings: 1   Prep time: 1 min

INGREDIENTS

·1 can sparkling water
·1 lemon wedge

DIRECTIONS

1. Pour sparkling water into a glass.
2. Add lemon wedge.
3. Serve immediately and enjoy!

CUCUMBER MINT INFUSED WATER

Servings: 1   Prep time: 5 min

INGREDIENTS

·1 cup water
·1/2 cucumber, sliced
·1/4 cup mint leaves

DIRECTIONS

1. Combine water, cucumber, and mint leaves in a jar.
2. Refrigerate for at least 1 hour.
3. Serve chilled and enjoy!

BERRY SMOOTHIE

Servings: 1   Prep time: 2 min

INGREDIENTS

·1 cup unsweetened almond milk

·1/2 cup berries (such as strawberries, blueberries, or raspberries)

·1/4 cup Greek yogurt

·1 tablespoon ground flaxseed

DIRECTIONS

1. Combine all ingredients in a blender.
2. Blend until smooth.
3. Serve immediately and enjoy!

GREEN SMOOTHIE

Servings: 1   Prep time: 10 min

INGREDIENTS

·1 cup unsweetened almond milk

·1/2 cup spinach

·1/2 banana

·1/4 avocado

·1 tablespoon ground flaxseed

DIRECTIONS

1. Combine all ingredients in a blender.
2. Blend until smooth.
3. Serve immediately and enjoy!

CHIA SEED PUDDING

Servings: 1   Prep time: 5 min

INGREDIENTS

·1/2 cup chia seeds

·1 cup unsweetened almond milk

·1/4 cup berries (such as strawberries, blueberries, or raspberries)

·1 tablespoon ground flaxseed

DIRECTIONS

1. Combine chia seeds, almond milk, berries, and flaxseed in a jar.
2. Stir to combine.
3. Cover jar and refrigerate for at least 4 hours, or overnight.
4. Stir before serving.

GOLDEN MILK

Servings: 1   Prep time: 5 min

INGREDIENTS

·1 cup unsweetened almond milk

·1/4 teaspoon turmeric powder

·1/4 teaspoon ground ginger

·1/4 teaspoon black pepper

DIRECTIONS

1. Combine all ingredients in a saucepan.
2. Heat over medium heat until warmed through, stirring occasionally.
3. Do not boil.
4. Pour into a mug and enjoy!

SPARKLCCCCE

Servings: 1   Prep time: 2 min

INGREDIENTS

·Sparkling water
·1-2 slices of fresh lime

DIRECTIONS

1. Add slices of fresh lime to sparkling water for a zesty and hydrating beverage

CCCCURMERIC TEA

Servings: 1   Prep time: 10 min

INGREDIENTS

·1 ginger tea bag
·1/2 tsp ground turmeric
·1 cup of hot water

DIRECTIONS

1. Steep the ginger tea bag in hot water and add ground turmeric for a soothing and anti-inflammatory tea

CCCCOTHIE

Servings: 1   Prep time: 5 min

INGREDIENTS

·1/2 cup frozen blueberries
·1 cup fresh spinach
·1/2 cup unsweetened almond milk

DIRECTIONS

1. Blend the blueberries, spinach, and almond milk for a nutrient-packed, low-carb smoothie

CHIA SEED AND LECCC

Servings: 1   Prep time: 5 min

INGREDIENTS

·1 tbsp chia seeds
·1/2 lemon, juiced
·1 cup of water

DIRECTIONS

1. Mix chia seeds, lemon juice, and water
2. Let it sit for a while to create a refreshing and fiber-rich beverage

SNACK

GREEK YOGURT AND BERRIES PARFAIT

Servings: 1   Prep time: 5 min   Cook time: /

INGREDIENTS

·1/2 cup plain Greek yogurt (unsweetened)

·1/2 cup mixed berries (e.g., blueberries, strawberries)

·1 tbsp chopped nuts (e.g., almonds or walnuts)

·1 tsp honey (optional, or use a sugar-free sweetener)

DIRECTIONS

1. Layer Greek yogurt and mixed berries in a bowl or glass
2. Top with chopped nuts
3. Drizzle with honey if desired

Cal per 100 g: 130   **Carbs: 18 g**   **Protein: 6 g**   **Fat: 5 g**

COTTAGE CHEESE AND SLICED CUCUMBER

Servings: 4   Prep time: 10 min   Cook time: 30 min

INGREDIENTS

·1/2 cup low-fat cottage cheese

·1 small cucumber, sliced

·Black pepper and a pinch of salt (optional)

DIRECTIONS

1. Serve cottage cheese with sliced cucumber
2. season with black pepper and a pinch of salt if desired

Cal per 100 g: 80   **Carbs: 4 g**   **Protein: 10 g**   **Fat: 3 g**

APPLE SLICES WITH ALMOND BUTTER

Servings: 1   Prep time: 5 min   Cook time: /

INGREDIENTS

·1 apple, sliced

·2 tbsp almond butter (unsweetened)

DIRECTIONS

1. Dip apple slices into almond butter for a satisfying and crunchy snack

Cal per 100 g: 170   **Carbs: 15 g**   **Protein: 5 g**   **Fat: 12 g**

CARROT AND HUMMUS SNACK

Servings: 1   Prep time: 10 min   Cook time: /

INGREDIENTS

·1 medium carrot, sliced into sticks

·2 tbsp hummus

DIRECTIONS

1. Dip carrot sticks into hummus for a fiber-rich and protein-packed snack

Cal per 100 g: 110   **Carbs: 110 g**   **Protein: 5 g**   **Fat: 7 g**

ROASTED CHICKPEAS

Servings: 4   Prep time: 5 min   Cook time: 25 min

INGREDIENTS

·2 cans (15 oz each) chickpeas, drained and rinsed

·2 tbsp olive oil

·1 tsp paprika

·1/2 tsp cumin

·1/2 tsp garlic powder

·Salt and pepper to taste

DIRECTIONS

1. Preheat your oven to 400°F (200°C)

2. Pat the chickpeas dry with a kitchen towel to remove excess moisture

3. In a bowl, toss the chickpeas with olive oil, paprika, cumin, garlic powder, salt, and pepper until well coated

4. Spread the chickpeas in a single layer on a baking sheet

5. Roast for about 25 minutes, or until they are crispy and golden brown

6. Let them cool before serving

Cal per 100 g: 172   Carbs: 42 g   Protein: 15 g   Fat: 15 g

HARD-BOILED EGGS

Servings: 2   Prep time: 10 min   Cook time: 10 min

INGREDIENTS

·4 large eggs

DIRECTIONS

1. Place eggs in a single layer in a saucepan.

2. Cover with cold water.

3. Bring to a boil over high heat.

4. Once boiling, cover and remove from heat.

5. Let eggs sit in hot water for 10 minutes.

6. Drain and immediately run cold water over eggs until cool.

7. Peel and enjoy!

Cal per 100 g: 165   Carbs: 0 g   Protein: 13 g   Fat: 11 g

YOGURT WITH BERRIES AND NUTS

Servings: 1   Prep time: 5 min   Cook time: /

INGREDIENTS

·1 cup plain Greek yogurt

·1/2 cup berries (such as strawberries, blueberries, or raspberries)

·1/4 cup nuts (such as almonds, walnuts, or pecans)

DIRECTIONS

1. In a bowl, combine yogurt, berries, and nuts.

2. Stir to combine.

3. Enjoy!

Cal per 100 g: 120   **Carbs: 15 g**   **Protein: 8 g**   **Fat: 4 g**

APPLE SLICES WITH PEANUT BUTTER

Servings: 1   Prep time: 10 min   Cook time: /

INGREDIENTS

·1 apple, sliced

·2 tablespoons peanut butter

DIRECTIONS

1. Spread peanut butter on apple slices.

2. Enjoy!

Cal per 100 g: 180   **Carbs: 15 g**   **Protein: 5 g**   **Fat: 20 g**

CARROT STICKS WITH HUMMUS

Servings: 1   Prep time: 5 min   Cook time: /

INGREDIENTS

·1 cup carrot sticks

·1/4 cup hummus

DIRECTIONS

1. Dip carrot sticks in hummus.
2. Enjoy!

Cal per 100 g: 90   **Carbs: 13 g**   **Protein: 5 g**   **Fat: 6 g**

CELERY STICKS WITH PEANUT BUTTER

Servings: 1   Prep time: 5 min   Cook time: /

INGREDIENTS

·1 cup celery sticks

·2 tablespoons peanut butter

DIRECTIONS

1. Spread peanut butter on celery sticks.

2. Enjoy!

Cal per 100 g: 80   **Carbs: 5 g**   **Protein: 5 g**   **Fat: 5 g**

EDAMAME

Servings: 4 **Prep time: 10 min** **Cook time: 30 min**

INGREDIENTS

·1 cup frozen edamame, in the pod

DIRECTIONS

1. Microwave edamame according to package directions.

2. Let cool slightly.

3. Remove edamame from the pod and enjoy!

Cal per 100 g: 120 **Carbs: 10 g** **Protein: 11 g** **Fat: 4 g**

BRUCHETTA

Servings: 4 **Prep time: 10 min** **Cook time: /**

INGREDIENTS

- 4 slices of thick crusty wholegrain bread
- Half a clove of garlic
- 2 teaspoons of olive oil
- 2 medium tomatoes

DIRECTIONS

- Take each slice of bread and cover lightly with half a teaspoon or so of olive oil
- Put the slices under the grill, taking care not to overcook them
- Hold the cut side of the garlic towards the bread and rub it lightly
- Chop some tomatoes and mix with olive oil
- Place loosely on top of the cooked bruschetta
- Eat and enjoy!

Cal per 100 g: 170 **Carbs: 24 g** **Protein: 7 g** **Fat: 5 g**

COURGETTE, FETA AND MINT SALAD

Servings: 2   Prep time: 10 min   Cook time: 12 min

INGREDIENTS

1 small courgette (100g)

Juice from ½ lemon

1 tsp olive oil

2 large handfuls rocket (80g)

25g Feta cheese, cubed

Large handful of mint, leaves chopped (25g)

DIRECTIONS

Preheat grill to medium-high.

Step 2

Cut the courgette into 0.5cm slices, toss in a bowl with 1tbsp lemon juice and 2tsp sunflower oil.

Step 3

Grill for 4-6 minutes each side, until lightly browned.

Step 4

Mix the courgette through the rocket, add the feta, season with black pepper to taste and serve.

Cal per serv. 69   Carbs: 2 g   Protein: 5 g   Fat: 5 g

SUMMER VEGETABLES WITH CITRUS DRESSING

Servings: 4   Prep time: 25 min   Cook time: 3 min

INGREDIENTS

100g fine beans, halved

3 baby courgettes/1 medium courgette, cut into chunks

150g broad beans, (shelled and skinned weight, or use frozen)

100g fresh/frozen peas

3 spring onions, sliced

2 tbsp coriander, chopped

1 tbsp pumpkin seeds, toasted

1 tsp olive oil

grated zest and juice 1 lime

DIRECTIONS

Place the fine beans into a pan of boiling water and cook for 2 minutes.

Add the courgettes, broad beans and peas and continue to cook for 1 minute. Drain and refresh under cold water, then transfer to a serving dish.

Mix together the remaining ingredients and toss through the vegetables. Serve.

Cal per 100 g: 102   Carbs: 8 g   Protein: 7 g   Fat: 5 g

To download, scan the QR code with your mobile phone.

FIND OUT THE MEAL PLAN

28 DAYS MEAL PLAN

Immerse yourself in a month-long culinary adventure with our meticulously crafted 28 Days Meal Plan. Say goodbye to mealtime monotony as you explore a diverse array of delicious and nutritious recipes, expertly designed to make every day a celebration of flavors and well-balanced nutrition.

DIABETIC SWEETS

Satisfy your sweet tooth without compromising on health with our Diabetic Sweets guide. Indulge in a collection of delectable treats that are thoughtfully crafted to meet the needs of those with diabetes. Discover the perfect balance of sweetness and health in every delightful recipe.

BONUS 1: A SIMPLE GUIDE TO READING FOOD LABELS

Food labels are an important tool for making informed food choices. They provide information about the nutritional composition of foods. They allow for comparing different products. They identify food additives. Learning to read food labels is an important skill that can help us make healthy food choices.

BONUS 2: <u>PRACTICAL GUIDE TO STARTING TRAINING</u>

Kickstart your fitness journey with confidence using our Practical Guide to Starting Training. Whether you're a beginner or returning to exercise, this guide provides expert insights, practical tips, and a structured approach to help you establish a sustainable and effective workout routine tailored to your individual needs. Check the guide at the end of the book.

BONUS 3: <u>MINDFULNESS AND RELAXTION TECHNIQUES</u>

Elevate your well-being with this guide." Delve into the transformative world of mindfulness, learning techniques to cultivate a present and peaceful state of mind. Uncover the power of mindfulness in enhancing your daily life, managing stress, and fostering a deeper connection with the world around you.

BONUS 4: <u>HIIT: THE BREAKTHROUGH WORKOUT</u>

Unleash the power of High-Intensity Interval Training (HIIT) with our guide to the breakthrough workout. Maximize your fitness gains in minimal time with efficient and dynamic workouts. Experience a new level of intensity and effectiveness, transforming your exercise routine and achieving results that speak volumes.

BONUS 5: <u>DIET JOURNAL</u>

Document your culinary journey and track your wellness progress with our 1 Year Food Journal. This invaluable companion allows you to record your recipes, meals, and fitness achievements, providing insight into your lifestyle choices over the course of a year. Stay motivated and organized on your path to a healthier and more mindful lifestyle.

ABOUT ME

Robert K. Edwards is a nutrition expert with over 10 years of experience in the fitness and health industry. He is the author of the book " THE COMPLETE DIABETIC DIET AFTER 50," which provides comprehensive information on how to manage diabetes through diet.

Robert has a passion for helping people live healthier lives, and he believes that nutrition is one of the most important factors in preventing and managing chronic diseases like diabetes. He is a firm believer in the power of food to heal, and he is committed to providing his readers with the information they need to make informed choices about their health.

He is also married and has two children, a son and a daughter. He loves spending time with his family and enjoys cooking healthy meals for them.

If you've enjoyed a book lately, could you leave a review on Amazon? Simply scan the QR code below with your phone's camera to share your thoughts. Your feedback helps fellow readers and supports the author.

Thank you!

GETTING STARTED

WITH FITNESS

INTRODUCTION

Welcome to "Fitness for Everyone: Getting Started Guide"! Thank you for choosing our guide to kickstart your fitness journey. Whether you're a complete beginner or looking to refresh your fitness routine, this guide is here to support you every step of the way.

Your Journey Begins Here In the pages that follow, you'll find practical advice, workout tips, and valuable information to help you embark on a successful fitness journey. I invite you to read attentively and take action on the guidance provided to unlock your full fitness potential. Remember, your journey starts now!

OVERVIEW OF EXERCISE

In this section, we'll explore the importance of exercise in your life and why it's a crucial component of your overall health and well-being.

The Significance of Exercise

Exercise isn't just about building muscles or losing weight; it's a key pillar of a healthy lifestyle. Regular physical activity has a profound impact on various aspects of your life, including:

1. **Physical Health:** Exercise helps maintain a healthy weight, strengthens your cardiovascular system, and reduces the risk of chronic illnesses such as heart disease, diabetes, and hypertension.

2. **Mental Well-Being:** Physical activity releases endorphins, your brain's natural mood lifters, which can reduce stress, anxiety, and symptoms of depression.

3. **Increased Energy:** Engaging in regular exercise can boost your energy levels, making you feel more alert and awake throughout the day.

4. **Improved Sleep:** Those who exercise regularly often experience better sleep quality, which is essential for overall health and vitality.

5. **Enhanced Longevity:** Studies consistently show that people who lead active lives tend to live longer and enjoy a higher quality of life in their later years.

BENEFITS AT ANY LEVEL

Whether you're new to fitness or returning after a hiatus, this guide is designed to cater to individuals of all fitness levels. The benefits of exercise are attainable for everyone, regardless of age, body type, or prior experience.

So, whether your goal is to lose weight, gain strength, boost your mood, or simply improve your overall health, remember that you're taking a significant step toward a healthier, happier you by delving into the world of fitness.

In the next pages, we'll guide you through the essentials of starting a safe and effective exercise routine, setting realistic fitness goals, and staying motivated along the way. Your journey to a healthier you begins here, so let's get started!

PREPARING TO BEGIN

Before you dive into your fitness journey, it's essential to make some initial preparations to ensure your safety and success. In this section, we'll explore what you should consider before you start your workout routine.

Understanding Your Current Health Status

Before you begin any exercise program, it's crucial to assess your current health status. Factors to consider include:

1. Medical Conditions: Are there any existing medical conditions or injuries that might affect your ability to exercise? Consult with your healthcare provider if you have any concerns.

2. Physical Limitations: Take stock of your current physical capabilities. This self-assessment will help you choose exercises that are appropriate for your fitness level.

3. Allergies or Sensitivities: If you have allergies or sensitivities, especially to food or environmental factors, be mindful of how they might affect your workouts and recovery.

Consulting with a Healthcare Professional

If you have any doubts about your ability to engage in physical activity or if you have any underlying health issues, it's wise to consult with a healthcare professional. They can provide tailored advice and ensure that your exercise plan aligns with your medical history.

Choosing the Right Environment

Consider the environment in which you plan to exercise:

- Gym: If you're heading to a gym, familiarize yourself with the equipment and facilities. Ask for a gym orientation if you're new.
- Home: If you prefer to work out at home, set up a designated workout space with adequate ventilation, lighting, and any necessary equipment.

Investing in Proper Gear

Having the right workout gear can make a significant difference in your comfort and safety. Depending on your chosen activities, you might need items like proper footwear, breathable clothing, or protective gear.

Setting Realistic Expectations

Remember, everyone's fitness journey is unique. Setting realistic expectations and understanding that progress takes time is essential. Be patient with yourself and focus on gradual improvement rather than immediate results.

By taking these preparatory steps, you're laying a solid foundation for your fitness journey. It's all about ensuring your safety, optimizing your experience, and setting yourself up for success as you progress through this guide. In the next pages, we'll delve into the process of goal setting, workout planning, and more, so stay tuned!

SETTING YOUR FITNESS GOALS

In your fitness journey, having clear and achievable goals is like having a roadmap; it helps you stay focused and motivated. This page explores the importance of setting your fitness goals and how to go about it.

Why Set Fitness Goals?

Fitness goals serve as your guiding star on this journey. They give you a sense of purpose and direction, making it easier to track your progress and stay committed. Here's why setting fitness goals is crucial:

1. Motivation: Goals provide motivation to start and continue exercising regularly. They give you a reason to lace up your sneakers and hit the gym or start that home workout.

2. Measurement: Having specific goals allows you to measure your progress objectively. You can see how far you've come and make necessary adjustments to your routine.

3. Focus: Goals help you concentrate on what's important. They prevent distractions and help you avoid wandering aimlessly through your fitness journey.

1. To set effective fitness goals, follow these steps:
2. Be Specific: Rather than a vague goal like "get in shape," be specific. For example, "lose 10 pounds in three months" or "run a 5K in under 30 minutes."
3. Make It Measurable: Use numbers or metrics to quantify your goals. This makes it easier to track progress. For example, "do 20 push-ups" or "reduce body fat by 5%."
4. Set Realistic Goals: While ambition is admirable, setting unrealistic goals can lead to frustration. Ensure your goals are attainable within your current circumstances.
5. Set a Timeline: Assign a timeframe to your goals. This adds a sense of urgency and helps you stay committed. For instance, "achieve my goal within six months."
6. Consider Your Preferences: Your goals should align with your interests and preferences. If you hate running, setting a goal to run a marathon may not be the best choice.
7. Break It Down: If your ultimate goal is significant, break it into smaller, manageable milestones. This makes the journey less overwhelming.

Remember, your fitness goals are personal to you. They should reflect what you want to achieve and why it matters to you. Whether your goals are weight-related, performance-based, or health-focused, they are essential motivators on your path to fitness success.

In the next pages, we'll guide you through the process of planning your workouts to align with your goals. Stay tuned for tips on creating a customized fitness routine that suits your objectives and fitness level!

PLANNING YOUR WORKOUT

Creating a well-structured workout plan is essential for a successful fitness journey. On this page, we'll delve into the details of planning your workouts, setting the foundation for a routine that aligns with your fitness goals.

The Importance of a Workout Plan

Think of your workout plan as the blueprint for your fitness journey. Having a structured plan:

1. **Ensures Consistency:** A plan helps you stay on track by providing a clear outline of what you need to do each day or week.
2. **Avoids Overtraining:** It prevents overexertion and burnout by spacing out different types of workouts and allowing for adequate rest.
3. **Optimizes Progress:** A well-designed plan focuses on your specific fitness goals, maximizing your chances of success.

Designing Your Workout Plan

Here's how to create a workout plan tailored to your needs:

1. **Define Your Goals:** Start by revisiting the fitness goals you set. Your plan should reflect these objectives, whether they involve weight loss, strength gain, or improved endurance.
2. **Choose Your Activities:** Select exercises and activities that align with your goals. For example, strength training for muscle building, cardio for weight loss, or yoga for flexibility.

- **Frequency and Duration:** Determine how often you'll work out each week and the duration of each session. Beginners might start with 3-4 days a week for 30-45 minutes per session.

- **Balance Your Routine:** Ensure your plan includes a mix of cardiovascular exercises, strength training, and flexibility work. This holistic approach improves overall fitness.

- **Progressive Overload:** Gradually increase the intensity or difficulty of your workouts as your fitness level improves. This principle promotes continued growth.

- **Rest Days:** Don't forget to schedule rest days. These are crucial for recovery and reducing the risk of overtraining.

- **Record Your Plan:** Write down your workout plan in a journal or use a fitness app to track your progress and make adjustments as needed.

Sample Workout Plan

Here's a simplified sample workout plan for someone new to fitness:
- **Monday:** 30 minutes of brisk walking or jogging
- **Tuesday:** Strength training (bodyweight exercises)
- **Wednesday:** Rest day
- **Thursday:** 30 minutes of cycling or swimming
- **Friday:** Strength training (dumbbell exercises)
- **Saturday:** Yoga or stretching routine
- **Sunday:** Rest day

Remember, this is just a starting point. Your workout plan should be personalized to fit your goals, fitness level, and lifestyle. In the following pages, we'll explore various workout types and exercises to help you build a plan that suits you best. Stay tuned for more guidance on your fitness journey!

TYPES OF WORKOUT

When it comes to fitness, variety is key. This page explores different types of workouts to help you choose the one that aligns with your goals and preferences.

Understanding Workout Variety

Exercise is not one-size-fits-all, and the type of workout you choose should match your goals, interests, and fitness level. Here are some popular workout types to consider:

- Cardiovascular (Cardio) Workouts: Cardio exercises increase your heart rate and breathing. They're excellent for burning calories, improving cardiovascular health, and boosting endurance. Examples include running, cycling, swimming, and dancing.

- **Strength Training:** Strength training involves resistance exercises that help build muscle mass and increase strength. It's essential for toning your body, improving metabolism, and enhancing functional fitness. You can use weights, resistance bands, or your body weight for resistance.

- **Flexibility and Mobility Workouts:** These workouts focus on improving joint flexibility and mobility. Yoga and Pilates are excellent options that help with balance, posture, and relaxation.

- **High-Intensity Interval Training (HIIT):** HIIT involves short bursts of intense exercise followed by brief rest periods. It's known for its efficiency in burning calories and improving cardiovascular fitness. HIIT workouts can vary widely in intensity and duration.

- **Functional Fitness:** Functional fitness exercises mimic movements used in everyday life, such as lifting, carrying, and squatting. They improve overall body strength and stability.

- **Mind-Body Practices:** Mind-body workouts like Tai Chi and Qigong combine physical activity with mental focus. They promote relaxation, balance, and a sense of well-being.

Choosing the Right Workout for You

When selecting a workout type, consider the following factors:

- **Your Goals:** If you aim to lose weight, cardio workouts may be your focus. If you want to build muscle, strength training is crucial.

- **Personal Preferences:** Choose workouts that you enjoy. If you dislike a particular activity, you're less likely to stick with it.

- **Fitness Level:** Start with workouts that match your current fitness level and gradually progress to more challenging ones.

- **Time Commitment:** Consider the time you can realistically devote to workouts each week.

- **Variety:** A balanced fitness routine often includes a mix of different workout types to target various aspects of fitness.

As you read through this guide, you'll find detailed information about each workout type, including exercises and tips for getting started. This knowledge will help you create a well-rounded fitness routine that's both effective and enjoyable. Your fitness journey is all about finding the right mix of activities that work best for you!

PROPER EXERCISE ESECUTION

Exercise is most effective when performed with the correct form and technique. On this page, we'll delve into the importance of proper exercise execution and provide tips on how to perform exercises safely and effectively.

Why Proper Form Matters

Executing exercises with proper form is essential for several reasons:

- **Injury Prevention:** Correct form minimizes the risk of injuries. It ensures that you're not placing unnecessary strain on joints or muscles.

- **Muscle Engagement:** Proper form targets the intended muscle groups more effectively, maximizing the benefits of each exercise.

- **Efficiency:** When you use proper form, you're more likely to achieve the desired results efficiently, saving time and effort.

- **Consistency:** Consistently using the right technique reinforces good habits and reduces the risk of developing bad ones.

Tips for Proper Exercise Form

Here are some general tips to help you maintain proper exercise form:

- **Start with the Basics:** If you're new to an exercise, begin with lighter weights or lower intensity to familiarize yourself with the movement.

- **Focus on Alignment:** Pay attention to your body's alignment during exercises. Keep your spine neutral, shoulders back, and core engaged.

-

- **Control the Movement:** Avoid using momentum to complete an exercise. Instead, focus on controlled, deliberate movements.

- **Breathe Properly:** Don't hold your breath during exercises. Inhale during the easier part of the movement and exhale during the more challenging phase.

- **Use a Mirror:** If possible, exercise in front of a mirror to check your form. It can help you identify and correct any misalignments.

- **Seek Guidance:** Consider working with a fitness professional, especially if you're new to exercise. They can provide personalized guidance and correct your form as needed.

Exercise-Specific Form Tips

- **For specific exercises, such as squats, lunges, or push-ups, it's crucial to understand the nuances of each movement. In this guide, you'll find detailed explanations and illustrations for proper form in various exercises.**

- **Remember that mastering proper form takes time and practice. It's more important to perform exercises correctly at a lower intensity than to rush into heavyweights or high-intensity workouts with poor form. As you progress on your fitness journey, continually focus on refining your technique to ensure safe and effective workouts.**

- **In the upcoming pages, you'll find guidance on different exercise types and specific form tips to help you achieve the best results while minimizing the risk of injury. Stay tuned for more valuable insights as you embark on your fitness adventure!**

TRACKING YOUR PROGRESS

Monitoring your fitness journey is a crucial part of achieving your goals. In this section, we'll explore the importance of tracking your progress and how to do it effectively.

Why Track Your Progress?

Tracking your progress offers several benefits:

- **Motivation:** It provides a sense of accomplishment as you see improvements in your strength, endurance, or body composition over time.
- **Accountability:** Tracking holds you accountable to your goals. When you record your progress, you're less likely to skip workouts or deviate from your plan.
- **Adjustment:** By analyzing your progress, you can make necessary adjustments to your workout routine and nutrition to keep moving towards your goals.
- **Identifying Patterns:** Tracking allows you to identify patterns, such as when you feel most energized for workouts or if certain exercises consistently lead to soreness.

Ways to Track Progress

Here are some effective ways to track your fitness progress:

- **Workout Journal:** Keep a journal to record each workout, including the exercises, sets, reps, and weights used. This provides a clear picture of your strength gains.
- **Before and After Photos:** Periodically take photos from different angles to visually track changes in your body composition.
- **Measurements:** Regularly measure key areas like your waist, hips, chest, and limbs. Document these measurements to track changes in body size.

- **Body Weight:** While not the sole indicator of progress, tracking your body weight can help you see overall trends.
- **Fitness Apps:** Use fitness apps or websites to log your workouts, nutrition, and other health data. Many apps provide graphs and charts to visualize your progress.
- **Fitness Tests:** Conduct fitness assessments, such as timed runs, bodyweight exercises, or flexibility tests, and record your results over time.

Setting Milestones

To make progress tracking more manageable and motivating, consider setting milestones:

- Short-term milestones (e.g., lifting a certain weight or running a specific distance).
- Mid-term milestones (e.g., losing a certain amount of body fat or achieving a fitness-related goal).
- Long-term milestones (e.g., reaching your ultimate fitness goal).

Celebrate your achievements when you reach these milestones to stay motivated and recognize your hard work.

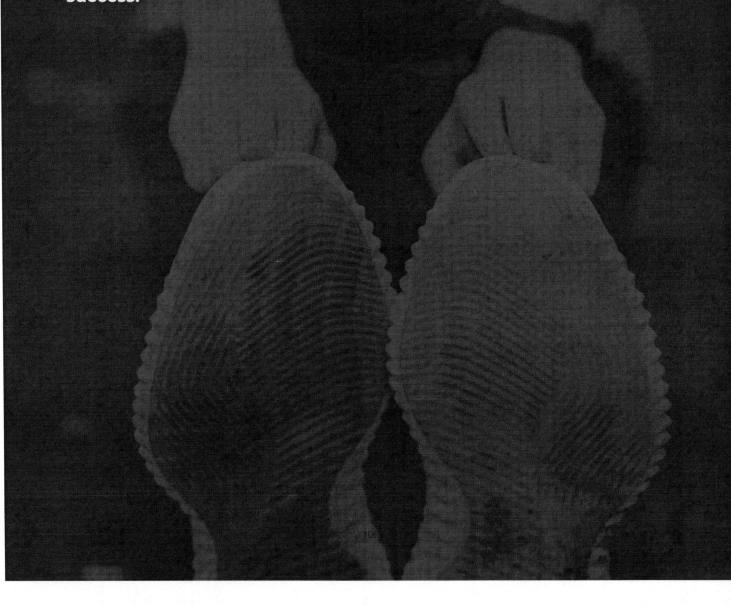

Analyzing Your Progress

- Periodically review your tracking data to analyze your progress. Look for patterns and trends, such as increases in strength, improved endurance, or changes in body composition. Based on your analysis, adjust your workout plan and goals as needed to continue making progress.

- In the following pages, we'll explore various tracking methods and provide additional tips on how to monitor your fitness journey effectively. Stay tuned as you continue your path toward fitness success!

NUTRITION AND RECOVERY

Achieving your fitness goals goes beyond exercise; it's closely intertwined with proper nutrition and adequate recovery. This page highlights the importance of a balanced diet and the role of recovery in your fitness journey.

Nutrition plays a significant role in your overall health and fitness. Proper nutrition provides the following benefits:

- **Fuel for Workouts:** The food you consume serves as your energy source during workouts, helping you perform at your best.
- **Muscle Recovery:** Adequate protein intake supports muscle repair and growth after exercise.
- **Weight Management:** A balanced diet contributes to maintaining a healthy weight, which is essential for achieving many fitness goals.
- **Nutrient Intake:** Proper nutrition ensures you get essential vitamins, minerals, and nutrients necessary for overall well-being.

Eating for Fitness Success

To make the most of your fitness journey, consider the following nutrition tips:

- **Balanced Diet:** Strive for a balanced diet that includes a variety of foods from all food groups, such as fruits, vegetables, lean proteins, whole grains, and healthy fats.
- **Pre-Workout Fuel:** Consume a light, balanced meal or snack 1-2 hours before exercise to provide energy.
- **Post-Workout Nutrition:** After a workout, refuel with a combination of protein and carbohydrates to aid in muscle recovery and replenish glycogen stores.
- **Stay Hydrated:** Drink plenty of water throughout the day to stay hydrated, especially during workouts.

- **Portion Control:** Be mindful of portion sizes to avoid overeating, and pay attention to hunger and fullness cues.
- **Limit Processed Foods:** Minimize the consumption of processed and sugary foods, which can hinder progress.

The Importance of Recovery

Recovery is an often-overlooked aspect of fitness that's crucial for long-term success. Adequate recovery:

- **Prevents Overtraining:** Proper rest between workouts helps prevent overtraining, reducing the risk of injuries and burnout.
- **Muscle Repair:** During rest, your body repairs and strengthens muscles, helping them grow and adapt.
- **Reduced Stress:** Adequate recovery contributes to reduced stress levels and overall well-being.
- **Improved Performance:** Rest days allow your body and mind to recharge, leading to better performance in subsequent workouts.

Prioritizing Rest and Sleep

Make sure to prioritize rest and sleep in your fitness routine:

- Aim for 7-9 hours of quality sleep per night to support muscle recovery and overall health.
- Incorporate rest days into your weekly workout schedule to allow your body to recover fully.

ADDITIONAL RESOURCES

To enhance your fitness journey and provide you with valuable support, we've compiled a list of additional resources that you can explore. These resources cover a wide range of topics related to fitness, nutrition, and overall well-being.

1. Online Fitness Communities

Joining online fitness communities or forums can be a great way to connect with like-minded individuals, seek advice, and share your progress. Here are a few popular online fitness communities to consider:

- **Reddit Fitness Subreddits:** Communities like r/Fitness and r/xxfitness provide a platform for discussions, questions, and fitness-related content.

- **MyFitnessPal Community:** This platform offers forums, groups, and a supportive community focused on nutrition and exercise.

2. Fitness Apps and Tools

There are numerous fitness apps and tools available that can help you track your workouts, plan meals, and stay motivated. Here are a few to explore:

- **MyFitnessPal:** This app allows you to track your diet and exercise, set goals, and connect with friends for accountability.

- **Fitbit:** If you own a Fitbit device, their app helps you track activity, sleep, and nutrition.

- **Strava:** Ideal for runners and cyclists, Strava lets you log and share your workouts while connecting with a community of athletes.

3. Online Workouts and Classes

Accessing online workouts and classes can add variety to your fitness routine and accommodate different preferences. Some popular platforms include:

- **YouTube Fitness Channels:** Many fitness experts offer free workout videos on YouTube, covering various fitness styles and levels.

- **Fitness Apps:** Apps like Nike Training Club, Daily Burn, and Beachbody On Demand provide a wide range of workouts led by certified trainers.

4. Blogs and Websites

Explore fitness blogs and websites for in-depth articles, tutorials, and expert advice on exercise, nutrition, and overall health. Some reputable sources include:

- **Bodybuilding.com:** A comprehensive resource for fitness articles, workout plans, and nutrition guidance.

- **Precision Nutrition:** Offers evidence-based nutrition advice and coaching services.

5. Podcasts

Fitness and health podcasts are a convenient way to gain knowledge and motivation while on the go. Here are a few popular options:

- **The Joe Rogan Experience:** Features interviews with experts in various fields, including fitness and nutrition.

- **The Model Health Show:** Hosted by Shawn Stevenson, this podcast covers a wide range of health and wellness topics.

6. Books and Ebooks

Consider exploring books and ebooks on fitness, nutrition, and personal development. You can find these at your local library, bookstore, or as digital downloads. Remember that your book, "Fitness for Everyone," is an excellent resource for comprehensive fitness guidance.

By tapping into these additional resources, you'll have a wealth of information and support to complement your fitness journey. Whether you're looking for inspiration, workout ideas, nutrition tips, or a sense of community, these resources can help you achieve your fitness goals.

In conclusion, your journey to a healthier and fitter you begins with the knowledge and insights shared in this guide. Remember that fitness is a personal journey, and what matters most is your commitment to progress. Stay dedicated, stay safe, and consult with a healthcare professional for personalized advice. With the right information and determination, you can achieve your fitness goals and enjoy a happier, healthier lifestyle. Start now, and embrace the rewarding path of fitness!

MEDICAL DISCLAIMER

The information provided in this guide is for informational purposes only and should not be considered as medical advice or a substitute for consultation with a qualified healthcare professional. The author and publisher of this guide are not medical professionals, and the content provided here is based on general knowledge and research available up to the knowledge cutoff date in September 2021.

It is essential to understand that every individual's health and fitness needs are unique, and what may be suitable for one person may not be appropriate for another. Always consult with a licensed healthcare provider or a qualified medical practitioner before making any significant changes to your diet, exercise routine, or lifestyle.

Manufactured by Amazon.ca
Acheson, AB